# The Loss of Western Civ

A report by the

**NATIONAL ASSOCIATION** *of* **SCHOLARS**

Stanley Kurtz
Senior Fellow, Ethics and Public Policy Center

ISBN: 978-0-9653143-2-9
Cover Design by Chance Layton
Interior Design by Beck & Stone and Chance Layton
© 2020 National Association of Scholars

# About the National Association of Scholars

## Mission

The National Association of Scholars is an independent membership association of academics and others working to sustain the tradition of reasoned scholarship and civil debate in America's colleges and universities. We uphold the standards of a liberal arts education that fosters intellectual freedom, searches for the truth, and promotes virtuous citizenship.

## What We Do

We publish a quarterly journal, *Academic Questions*, which examines the intellectual controversies and the institutional challenges of contemporary higher education.

We publish studies of current higher education policy and practice with the aim of drawing attention to weaknesses and stimulating improvements.

Our website presents educated opinion and commentary on higher education, and archives our research reports for public access.

NAS engages in public advocacy to pass legislation to advance the cause of higher education reform. We file friend-of-the-court briefs in legal cases defending freedom of speech and conscience and the civil rights of educators and students. We give testimony before congressional and legislative committees and engage public support for worthy reforms.

NAS holds national and regional meetings that focus on important issues and public policy debates in higher education today.

## Membership

NAS membership is open to all who share a commitment to its core principles of fostering intellectual freedom and academic excellence in American higher education. A large majority of our members are current and former faculty members. We also welcome graduate and undergraduate students, teachers, college administrators, and independent scholars, as well as non-academic citizens who care about the future of higher education.

NAS members receive a subscription to our journal *Academic Questions* and access to a network of people who share a commitment to academic freedom and excellence. We offer opportunities to influence key aspects of contemporary higher education.

Visit our website, www.nas.org, to learn more about NAS and to become a member.

# Con

11 ——————————————————

17 ——————————————————

73 ——————————————————

95 ——————————————————

147 —————————————————

Introduction

Part One: Failed Disbelief

Part Two: How the West Was Lost

Part Three: Accusation and Its Discontents

Index

# Introduction

## Introduction

America is divided today. Ideologically, we are split as we were when blue and gray armies faced off at Bull Run, though so far no armies have emerged to back the vitriolic rhetoric indulged in by both sides in our emerging "cold civil war." The Civil War of 1861-1865 emerged from the national debate over slavery. The cold civil war we have today emerged, oddly enough, on college campuses.

In January of 1987, students at Stanford University chanting "Hey hey, ho ho, Western Culture's got to go," kicked off this culture war. The fissure that opened three decades ago at Stanford—between the new multicultural way, on the one hand, and traditional American conceptions of history and citizenship, on the other—has widened now into a chasm.

What began as a colorful political side-show grew in the years that followed to become the script of our politics. The divisions that tore Stanford apart then now generate America's most important political and cultural controversies. And Stanford remains an excellent place to study the origins and the likely future course of our growing national divisions.

This report returns to Stanford in 1987, and follows the controversy's forgotten threads back to the beginnings of American history and forwards to today. Today's radical student activism is rooted in powerful intellectual currents injected into university life several decades ago. Those currents in the American academy were skeptical, relativist, historicist, and even nihilist in character. The connections to today's student activists are direct, but obscured by a seeming paradox. How does the radical skepticism of one generation—its indulgence in comprehensive disbelief—become another generation's blinding moral certainty? How did deconstructionist skepticism lay the groundwork for the omni-directional accusations of racism and bigotry that seem to have swallowed not only today's college students but American politics as a whole?

The Western tradition is the source of America's founding principles and constitutional system. That is the most important reason for civic-minded citizens to study it. And while America has been shaped by the particularities of Western civilization, the liberal principles nurtured by this tradition represent our best hope for national reconciliation across boundaries of race, ethnicity, and religion. This report can be read as an argument against those on either the right or the left who associate Western civilization with "white identity politics." The distinctive idea that emerged in the West—to be taken up into what we used to call the American Creed—is that a polity based on the principles of liberty and equality belongs to all citizens, as individuals, regardless of race, faith, ethnicity, or national origin. This is the way out of the trap we have fallen into. How we lost our way is the subject of this report.

We begin in Part One by critiquing a landmark of modern historical deconstructionism: the claim that the very idea of Western civilization is a modern invention devised during World War I as a way of hoodwinking young American soldiers into fighting and dying in the trenches of Europe. This thesis, propounded in 1982 by the historian Gilbert Allardyce, was cited by key players during the original Stanford controversy. Those scholars used Allardyce to show that elimination of Stanford's required course on the history and literature of the West was not a major break with the past.

In the decades since the Stanford dustup, the Allardyce thesis has been invoked to justify the replacement of college and K-12 Western Civilization courses with World History, or with heavily globalized versions of European and American history. The Allardyce thesis shows how a wildly improbable bit of scholarly radicalism virtually unknown to the general public can nonetheless sweep the academy and transform American education. The Allardyce thesis is also an early and influential example of the sort of debunking continually churned out by historians nowadays, yet almost never itself subject to critical scrutiny. It's time the debunkers were debunked.

A proper critique of Allardyce requires nothing less than an excavation of the lost history of Western civilization. Allardyce argues that, prior to World War I, American college students never truly studied the West. That may sound implausible, but Allardyce marshals significant evidence to make his case. To expose his errors, we'll need to recover the lost story of America's college humanities curriculum from the colonial period through the First World War. In the process, we'll rediscover some great and long-forgotten historians of the West, people like William Robertson and Francois Guizot, and a portion of what they have to teach us today.

In Part Two, we'll consider the academic work of the scholars who invoked Allardyce to justify the elimination of Stanford's Western Culture requirement. That work foreshadowed and helped precipitate our current national divisions. In examining the academic work of Allardyce's acolytes, the follies and incoherence of multiculturalist, deconstructionist, and globalist history will be on full display.

Finally, in Part Three we'll return to Stanford, reviewing the Western Culture battle of 1987-88 from a new perspective, and considering as well a noble but failed student-led effort to restore Stanford's Western Civ requirement in 2016. This review will amount to a tour of modern multiculturalism and its latest incarnation, "intersectionality." What, we shall ask, has happened at Stanford since 1987, and what can the continuities and changes tell us about where America is headed now? We'll pursue these questions, in part, by reconsidering Allan Bloom's sensational 1987 bestseller, *The Closing of the American Mind*, which many believe predicted the Stanford Western Culture controversy, and which quickly became enmeshed in that battle. Bloom's insights are alive today, though in an environment he did not entirely foresee.

The upshot of this tour will be a new way of looking at the present. We'll argue, among other things, that: 1) Postmodern academic skepticism, and the broader collapse of faith it reflects, has backed us into a corner in which inflated accusations of racism, bigotry, and genocide are virtually the only remaining sources of collective purpose; 2) Postmodern academic skepticism has become a petrified orthodoxy every bit as due for critique as the Aristotelianism of Hobbes's day; 3) So-called multiculturalism isn't really about preserving traditional cultures at all—instead "multiculturalism" has ushered in a radically new sort of culture in which perpetually expanding accusations of racism, bigotry, and genocide stand as quasi-religious ends in themselves; and 4) The American experiment cannot survive without checking or reversing these trends.

As this report goes to press, Stanford's ever-changing humanities core is about to enter a new phase. Should Stanford's Faculty Senate approve, a proposed new three-quarter requirement in "civic education and global citizenship" will go into effect in the 2020-21 academic year.[1] On an optimistic view, the proposed change was precipitated or hastened by the 2016 student-led campaign to restore Western Civ. The new core significantly increases the amount of humanities coursework

---

1  Leily Rezvani, "Stanford Core: Faculty proposes new first-year requirement focused on civic education," *The Stanford Daily*, September 24, 2019, https://www.stanforddaily.com/2019/09/24/stanford-core-faculty-proposes-new-first-year-requirement-focused-on-civic-education/

required of Stanford students. And despite its reference to "global education," courses covering more traditional topics will no doubt be included under the new requirement's umbrella.

On a more cynical view, the new proposal is an attempt to climb out of the enrollment-hole into which humanities departments have dug themselves by recourse to postmodern theory. As David Randall's "Making Citizens" report for NAS has shown, moreover, "civic education" is the anodyne camouflage behind which modern universities often introduce coursework in progressive political activism.[2] A requirement in "global citizenship," of course, is the apotheosis of the dismaying trends outlined in this report, and the antithesis of traditional Western Civ.

Time will tell which of these two readings carries more weight. In any case, the furies set loose by Stanford's original Western Culture controversy have long since worked their way into our body politic. They will not soon disappear.

---

2  David Randall, *Making Citizens: How American Universities Teach Civics*, (New York: National Association of Scholars, 2017), https://nas.org/storage/app/media/Reports/Making%20Citizens/NAS_makingCitizens_full-Report.pdf

# Part One: Failed Disbelief

## Part One: Failed Disbelief

For sixteen years now, John Lennon's song, "Imagine," has been played or sung just before the ball drops on New Year's Eve in New York City's Times Square.[3] This fledgling ritual tradition tells us a great deal about what we might call the secular political religion of modernity. "Imagine there's no countries; it isn't hard to do; nothing to kill or die for; and no religion too."

Although the sentiment is widespread, it is by no means uncontested. Adherence to Lennon's creed is arguably now the central dividing line in American cultural politics. On the other side of that line lies a sense that America has been unjustly neglected in everything from its workers, to its borders, to its great and distinctive spirit.

Along with this determination to revive America goes dismay over the neglect of Western Civilization, that long and great cultural and historical tradition of which America is said to be a singular exemplar and an essential bulwark. Although President Trump invoked Western Civilization and the need to defend it in his widely discussed 2017 speech in Warsaw, regard for Western Civilization has not been much evident of late in our ceremonies, our oratory, or our schools.[4]

January of 2017 marked the 30th anniversary of the famous protest at which Stanford University students chanted, "Hey hey, ho ho, Western culture's got to go."[5] Those students were aiming to dismantle Stanford's required course on the history and great works of Western Civilization. They not only succeeded but helped set off a "multiculturalist" movement that swept away Western Civilization courses at most American colleges and set the terms of our cultural battles for decades to come.[6]

Nearly 30 years out from Stanford's consequential decision, it seemed as though the era of Western Civilization had well and truly passed, replaced by the ethos of globalizing multiculturalism. Then in 2016 came the return of the repressed, as the West, the nation-state, and the idea of America rushed back to grapple with the cosmopolitan foe.

---

3   "Imagine (John Lennon Song," at Wikipedia, https://en.wikipedia.org/wiki/Imagine_(John_Lennon_song).
4   Donald Trump, "Here's the Full Text of Donald Trump's Speech in Poland," NBC News, July 6, 2017, https://www.nbcnews.com/politics/donald-trump/here-s-full-text-donald-trump-s-speech-poland-n780046.
5   Richard Bernstein, "In Dispute on Bias, Stanford is Likely to Alter Western Culture Program," *The New York Times*, Jan. 19, 1988, https://www.nytimes.com/1988/01/19/us/in-dispute-on-bias-stanford-is-likely-to-alter-western-culture-program.html.
6   The complex trajectory of Western Civ's decline on campuses is difficult to trace. As this report shows, Stanford actually abolished a Western Civ-style course more than once. For more on the decline of college Western Civ courses, see Glenn Ricketts, Peter W. Wood, Stephen H. Balch, Ashley Thorne, *The Vanishing West: 1964-2010*, (New York: National Association of Scholars, 2011, https://www.nas.org/storage/app/media/images/documents/TheVanishingWest.pdf).

Although it's too soon to predict the outcome of this struggle, a lesson does suggest itself. Something at the core of globalizing multiculturalist thinking underestimates the persistence and solidity—indeed, the very reality—of its national and civilizational antagonists. Advocates of globalizing multiculturalism tend to treat human social reality as an infinitely malleable construction, something essentially imagined into existence, and therefore capable of being more or less easily wished away. Thus the allure for academics of ideas like "invented traditions" and "imagined communities," conceptual tools designed to subvert and dissolve the apparent reality of nations, cultures, and civilizations, and also the conviction on the part of many Europeans that the lofty political goals behind the common currency could obviate very real divergences between Europe's national economies, thus as well Chancellor Merkel's conviction that an enthusiastic "we can do this," would overcome the cultural gulf between Europe and the Middle East.[7]

Belief in the necessity of transcending divisions of nation, culture, and civilization appears to entail suspicion about the very reality of these things. Conversely, the more real and recalcitrant nations, cultures, and civilizations turn out to be, the more suspiciously we might regard programs for their ultimate transcendence.

## Broken Shackles

We can test this issue by returning to the dispute that effectively kicked off the conflict between the traditional vision of America-in-the-West and the globalizing multiculturalist challenge: Stanford's 1987-88 battle over its required Western Culture course. At the time, advocates for dropping the requirement argued that the very idea of Western culture—and perhaps by implication Western Civilization itself—was largely an illusion. While this claim was one of many in the broader public debate, it was absolutely central to the way America's scholars understood the issue.

After that Stanford battle, the idea that Western Civilization—or at least our traditional regard for it—is a latter day "invention" became the

---

7   Benedict Anderson, *Imagined Communities: Reflections on the Origin and Spread of Nationalism*, (London: Verso, 1983); Eric Hobsbawm and Terence Ranger, *The Invention of Tradition*, (Cambridge; Cambridge University Press, 1983).

paradigm for a still-growing wave of *deconstructionist* history—a version of history that aims to debunk and overthrow the foundational narratives of America and the wider West.

This way of thinking—this suspicion cast on the reality of nation, culture, and civilization—is rarely itself subject to examination and critique. Yet it underlies the project of globalizing multiculturalism and accounts for much of its weakness. The conviction that Western Civilization is merely an "invented tradition" is an awesome and venerable idol in the temple of deconstructionist history. That idol is ripe for smashing.

To test this foundational deconstructionist claim and mark the lesson for our present dilemmas, we shall need to recover the lost history of Western Civilization. A civilization attains the ability to judge and guide itself by means of its history. Yet our civilizational history has been lost—above all the history of history itself. That is to say, the story of how the West has understood its own development has been lost. A look at courses on Western Civilization as they have been taught for America's first 150 years will help us make sense of what has happened to our country in the decades since Western Civ was banished from the academy. To reclaim the lost history of America's Western Civilization courses is to recover an understanding of who we are and what we have become. To do so, however, we shall have to burst the mental shackles forged by today's historians.

Let us return to "Imagine," because the easiest way to understand the program of contemporary academic historians is to think of it as one radical step beyond John Lennon: "Imagine there's no countries. It isn't hard to do: nothing to kill or die for, and no religion too." Academic history as currently written and taught is largely a brief for globalization. The idea is to undermine the public's sense of national or civilizational identity. With nothing left to kill or die for, the world will presumably "live as one."

While imagining a future without countries is "easy if you try," deconstructionist historians have the vastly more difficult task of imagining a world in which nations and civilizations have never truly existed to begin with. This seemingly impossible revision of the past is the one great leap historians take beyond "Imagine." Yet it may be the only way to achieve Lennon's goal. A people is bound by its shared sense of history. Disguise or abandon that history and you just might be able to dissolve your society and exchange it for a globalist alternative. But how do you imagine a past without nations or civilizations?

Here is where deconstruction comes in. Older historians understood themselves to be studying and describing actual societies. Contemporary historians, by contrast, tend to see their task as dispelling delusions of national and civilizational identity. For deconstructionist historians, every collective boundary-line is a flawed human construction susceptible to debunking, and especially deserving of such treatment when it encourages in-group identity—above all, war—at the expense of an "Other." For deconstructionist historians, the only sound and fully legitimate identity is a global identity. So it's actually easy to imagine a past without countries, because nations and civilizations were merely imaginary to begin with.

## Word Games

But are historians' deconstructive techniques at all persuasive? Consider a common strategy we might call "fun with maps." Instead of focusing on early American history, scholars now present colonial America as part of a broader "Atlantic World" built around the triangular exchange of goods between Africa, Europe, and the Americas.[8] This global perspective has the advantage for leftist historians of diverting attention from the democratic and religious reasons for the founding of New England, while turning the exploitative capitalism of the southern slave trade into the focus of early American history. Similarly, Europe's fuzzy eastern boundary allows it to be reimagined as a mere peninsular extension of Eurasia, which after all is united by the Indo-European language family.[9]

It all depends on what you think is important. We used to believe that individual liberty, religious freedom, liberal democracy, free markets, constitutionalism, scientific rationality, and the rule of law were significant enough to justify a focus on the traditions that created

---

8   Mike Henry, "Teaching About the Atlantic World," at AP Central by the College Board, https://apcentral.collegeboard.org/courses/ap-united-states-history/classroom-resources/teaching-about-atlantic-world.
9   Ian Almond, "Five Ways of Deconstructing Europe," *Journal of European Studies*, Vol. 44(1), 2014, pp. 50-63; Peter Burke, "How to Write a History of Europe: Europe, Europes, Eurasia," *European Review*, Vol. 14, No. 2, 2006, pp. 233-239; J. G. A. Pocock, "Some Europes in Their History," in Anthony Pagden, ed., *The Idea of Europe: From Antiquity to the European Union*, (Washington: Woodrow Wilson Center Press, 2002), pp. 55-62.

them—traditions that originated in the biblical and classical worlds, then developed through the Christian Middle Ages and the Europe of the Enlightenment, and finally spread to America and beyond. This was the core idea of Western Civilization as it flourished in the mid-20th century.[10] Deconstructionism is less a way of rebutting this idea than a strategy for ignoring it.

The granddaddy of all deconstructive techniques—let's call it "word games"—played a central role in the Western Civilization battle at Stanford. And as noted, it wields a powerful influence over historians to this day. The word game lets you debunk supposedly ancient traditions by tracing down their most recent name. Once you figure out whose interests the new name plays to, you can junk the supposedly hoary old tradition as a self-serving modern "invention."[11] So, for example, in 2016, UCLA's Lynn Hunt, a prominent globalist historian, announced in *Time Magazine* that "'Western civilization' was invented during World War I as a way of explaining to American soldiers why they were going to fight in Europe."[12]

Hunt was relying on an enormously influential 1982 article by Gilbert Allardyce that fingers not Periclean Athens or biblical Israel but the War Issues Course of the World War I Student Army Training Corps as the actual birthplace of Western Civilization.[13] The War Issues Course, explains Allardyce, taught an America once steeped in the idea of its own uniqueness to accept an alternative identity, this one highlighting the liberal democratic traditions we share with Europe. Thus did a wartime course designed to supply American soldiers with reasons to fight for our European allies inspire the mandatory "Western Civilization" surveys that spread across the country after World War I. Those classes flourished until the War in Vietnam, expressions of the alliance of the North Atlantic nations and their dominant position in the world. In sum, the Allardyce thesis suggests that Western Civilization is both a recent invention and a thinly disguised form of neo-imperial war propaganda.

Note how effectively the Allardyce thesis soothes the guilt of a Vietnam generation that saw nothing in Western Civilization worth

---

10  James Kurth, "Western Civilization, Our Tradition," *The Intercollegiate Review*, Fall2003/Spring 2004, pp. 5-13.
11  Pocock, "Some Europes in Their History," p. 55.
12  Lily Rothman, "The Problem with Rep. Steve King's Take on the Superiority of Western Civilization," *Time Magazine*, July 19, 2016, http://time.com/4413537/steve-king-subgroup-western-civilization/.
13  Gilbert Allardyce, "The Rise and Fall of the Western Civilization Course," *The American Historical Review*, Volume 87, Issue 3, June 1982, pp. 695-725.

fighting for. Perhaps, then, the new deconstructive and globalist histories are themselves forms of pacifist propaganda. Why bother defending an invention?

For decades, the Allardyce thesis has been adopted and elaborated by academic historians, most notably in Lawrence Levine's 1996 book, *The Opening of the American Mind*.[14] Levine's *Opening* was widely hailed as the Academy's definitive rebuttal of *The Closing of the American Mind*, Allan Bloom's best-selling 1987 brief for the great books of Western Civilization.[15] "The best response to critics of the modern American university," began Levine, "is the history of the university itself."[16]

Levine tells the story of the exclusion of medieval and modern history from the classical Greek and Latin curriculum that dominated America's universities until roughly the 1870s. Even ancient history received little serious attention in the 19th century, says Levine, since mindless drills in Latin grammar and deadening memorization exercises were the order of the day. Levine also describes the shift in American thinking from the exceptionalism of the 18th and 19th centuries to the very different 20th century belief in a common Western civilization. So, for example, Levine quotes John Adams warning Thomas Jefferson against importing European professors for his new University of Virginia. Then Levine highlights Jefferson's fears that European immigrants might fail to understand or appreciate America's democratic principles.[17]

Making a point tirelessly repeated by multiculturalist historians ever since, Levine concludes: "The Western Civ curriculum, portrayed by conservative critics of the university in our time as apolitical and of extremely long duration, was in fact neither. It was a 20th century phenomenon which had its origins in a wartime government initiative, and its heyday lasted for scarcely fifty years."[18]

Yet the Allardyce thesis is mistaken, and dramatically so. It's time the debunkers were debunked. American colleges and universities have been teaching Western Civilization since before the Revolution. The very idea of American exceptionalism makes no sense without the complementary idea of Western civilization. Yes, there's a relationship

---

14  Lawrence W. Levine, *The Opening of the American Mind: Canons, Culture, and History*, (Boston: Beacon Press, 1996), pp. 37-74.
15  Allan Bloom, *The Closing of the American Mind: How Higher Education Has Failed Democracy and Impoverished the Souls of Today's Students*, (New York: Simon and Schuster, 1987).
16  Levine, *The Opening of the American Mind*, p. 37.
17  Ibid., pp. 60-61.
18  Ibid., p. 73.

between war and Western civilization, but it's far less straightforward than Allardyce suggests. And the stereotype of the mind-deadening 18th and 19th century American college curriculum turns out to be a condescending exaggeration. Instead of dissing them, we should be learning from our often wiser forebears who we are.

Remarkably, the evidence needed to bust up the Allardyce thesis has been ready to hand all along. Our Lennonist historians simply haven't wanted to find it.

## Christendom

Americans have probed, praised, and pondered our civilizational antecedents from the start. The colonists adopted the classical curriculum in the first place because they believed the Renaissance revival of ancient learning had prepared the way for the Protestant Reformation.[19] True, these developments were understood as episodes in the history of "Christendom," rather than "Western Civilization." The difference of wording is important, too, since Christian histories placed God at the center, in contrast to the more secular civilizational histories that followed.

Jonathan Edwards, the leading figure of America's Great Awakening, preached a series of sermons in 1739 that surveyed all of history from creation through the anticipated return of Christ. Published posthumously in the 1770s, *A History of the Work of Redemption* is foundational to American Protestant thought.[20]

One of Edwards' innovations in that book was to integrate landmark moments in what would someday be called the story of Western civilization (such as the conversion of Constantine, the fall of Rome, the defeat of the Spanish Armada, the invention of the printing press, and the rise of Enlightenment deism) into the traditional biblical and end-times narrative. Reformation thinkers had long seen political actors as agents in God's redemptive plans, yet none had produced a history along these lines. In effect, Edwards was answering secular Enlightenment historians with a narrative built around God's work among the nations.[21]

---

19  Caroline Winterer, *The Culture of Classicism: Ancient Greece and Rome in American Intellectual Life*, 1780-1910, (Baltimore: The Johns Hopkins University Press, 2002), p. 10.

20  Jonathan Edwards, *A History of the Work of Redemption*, (Worcester: Isaiah Thomas, 1808 [1774]); George M. Marsden, *Jonathan Edwards: A Life*, (New Haven: Yale University Press, 2003), pp. 193-200, 263-267, 481-489.

21  Avihu Zakai, *Jonathan Edwards's Philosophy of History: The Reenchantment of the World in the Age of Enlightenment*, (Princeton: Princeton University Press, 2003), pp. 142-143.

And while Edwards spoke of Christendom, he also sometimes used the phrase "civilized nations" as a synonym. (The noun "civilization" had not yet been coined.)

Edwards understood New England's spiritual awakening as the dawning of a long, tumultuous end-times era. His vision of America's colonies as the cutting edge of global salvation history makes Edwards a classic American exceptionalist. Yet Edwards had an uncanny ability to make his listeners understand their most personal struggles as climactic episodes in an epic clash between the forces of God and Satan, a clash playing out from biblical days through the Roman Empire, the Reformation, and Europe's religious wars and revivals. Placing listeners at the climax of Christianity's far-flung history gave Edwards' sermons tremendous power.

Nor has American exceptionalism ever made sense apart from the story of Europe's struggles. John Winthrop's early Puritan "City on a Hill" was built for European eyes, its example offered as a redemptive antidote to the continent's infirmities.[22] American exceptionalism is essentially a story of descent and departure from Europe. The only way to understand America, then, is by reference to European history.

Jonathan Edwards died in 1758, not long after assuming the presidency of Princeton. Higher education had been for him a way of broadening and deepening America's spiritual awakening, with Christian history central to that effort. Yet within a decade Princetonians would be studying European civilization in a more modern and secular sense, and under a new name.

Toward the end of the 17th century, the term "Christendom" was gradually replaced by "Europe." German jurist Samuel von Pufendorf's best-selling and widely translated introduction to "Europe's" history was published in 1680. Gazettes of "Europe" carrying news of the continent's major cities emerged at that time as well. The 1714 Treaty of Utrecht, ending the War of the Spanish Succession, was the last European treaty to speak of "the Christian Republic" or "the Provinces of Christendom."[23]

As Europe emerged from its wars of religion, a secularizing shift had begun. And two centuries into the age of exploration, serious studies of China, Japan, India, and Africa were emerging, these on top of the

---

22   John Winthrop, "A Modell of Christian Charity," 1630, https://liberalarts.utexas.edu/coretexts/_files/resources/texts/1630 Model of Christian Charity.pdf
23   M.E. Yapp, "Europe in the Turkish Mirror," Past & Present, No. 137, Nov., 1992, p. 142.

struggles with the Ottoman Empire that followed the Islamic conquest of Constantinople in 1453.[24] Europe was coming to see itself as a whole, distinct from the rest of the world not only in religion, but in customs, economy, mode of government, and more.

So had Europe just been "invented?" Not really. The premise of the invention idea is that social life has no existence independent of the concepts through which we construct and contemplate it. So a name change is everything, and the very idea of civilizational continuity is deemed illusory from the start.

But how could modern Europe have recognized itself as a particular civilization in comparison to others had there not been something distinctive about it in the first place—manners, customs, and institutions slowly shaped by the classical and Christian heritage of previous centuries? You can't conjure away culture and history with a language game. Deconstructionism amounts to a cheap philosopher's trick for denying the force of traditions that have wrongly come to embarrass too many of us.

## Civilization

Nonetheless, the transition from "Christendom" to "Europe" was significant. And if anyone could be said to have "invented" not Europe itself, but the emerging modern conception of European civilization, it was Charles Louis de Secondat, baron de la Brede et de Montesquieu, who did it 170 years before the First World War.[25]

Montesquieu is famed as the Enlightenment thinker whose 1748 work, *The Spirit of the Laws*, bequeathed to America's Founders the principle of the separation of powers. Yet *The Spirit of the Laws* was also the first systematic comparative study of world civilizations.[26] By articulating a disciplined contrast with Asia, Montesquieu became the first modern thinker to set out a systematic vision of Europe as a cultural and political entity with a history of its own.[27]

---

24  Ibid., pp. 134-155.
25  Although Montesquieu was the first to explore and highlight the Europe/Asia contrast in a modern context, the idea of a democratic West versus a despotic East dates back to the father of history, Herodotus, in the 5th Century BC.
26  Montesquieu, *The Spirit of the Laws*, translated and edited by Anne M. Cohler et al., (Cambridge: Cambridge University Press, 1989).
27  Yapp, "Europe in the Turkish Mirror," p. 147; A helpful general treatment of Montesquieu's comparative approach can be found in Alan Macfarlane, "Montesquieu and the Making of the Modern World" a downloadable electronic book at http://www.alanmacfarlane.com/TEXTS/Montesquieu_final.pdf. This reprints the first part of Alan Macfarlane, *The Riddle of the Modern World: Of Liberty, Wealth and Equality*, (Houndmills: Macmillan Press Ltd., 2000).

With China, Japan, India, the Near East, Turkey and Russia ruled by 'despotic' regimes, Montesquieu saw that political liberty was confined to Western Europe. To explain that liberty, he referenced the character of Christianity, the social effects of commerce, the relative separation of religion and state, and the rule of law. In short, Montesquieu developed the core themes of a typical 20th century Western Civilization course in 1748.

He was also preoccupied by England's differences from Europe as a whole: its passion for liberty, its religious freedom and the proliferation of sects this gave rise to, as well as the cultural impact of its remarkably advanced commerce. England for Montesquieu played the "exceptional" role that America (or the Anglo-American tradition) took on in later narratives of Western Civilization.

Contemporary historians are quick to dismiss Montesquieu's treatment of "Oriental despotism," and it's true that he was better at noticing how Asian societies were unlike Europe than at grasping cultural features that softened the character of their "despotisms." Nonetheless, Montesquieu identified barriers to non-Western democratic development that remain powerful to this day: the treatment of women in the Islamic world, for example.[28]

Montesquieu was also far more critical of the West than he is often given credit for. Writing under the censorship of the French monarchy, Montesquieu could not be as bold in highlighting the dangers of Western despotism as he could be when discussing the East. Indeed he sometimes used his accounts of non-Western societies as a veiled way of suggesting the dangers of despotic abuse at home. And while he marked Christianity's role in abolishing Western slavery, softening the treatment of political foes, and reducing the subordination of women, he also noted ways in which Christianity could be abused to justify the burning of heretics or the enslavement of colonial subjects.[29] For all that, however, Montesquieu did suggest significant distinctions between the West and other societies based on factors like law, commerce, and Christianity. And while he saw the West as far from immune to despotism, it was the locale in which liberty had made its foremost appearance.

---

28  Montesquieu, *Spirit of the Laws*, p. 270.
29  Vickie B. Sullivan, *Montesquieu and the Despotic Ideas of Europe: An Interpretation of the Spirit of the Laws*, (Chicago: University of Chicago Press, 2017).

Montesquieu also sketched out themes soon to be elaborated in the civilizational histories that captured America's attention in the 18th and 19th centuries, histories the Allardyce thesis ignores. At base, these themes involve the character of Europe's uniquely dispersed and conflicting cultural and political power-centers.

Although Montesquieu was the first thinker to systematically characterize "Europe," the word "civilization" hadn't yet been coined in 1748. "Spirit" came close, since Montesquieu used it to summarize the totality of factors that shaped the laws of a given world-region. Montesquieu may be indirectly responsible for "civilization," though; it was a French disciple of his who first coined the term in 1757, after which it swiftly became popular.[30]

Civilization was an idea whose time had come. The pace of change was quickening in the run-up to the French and Industrial revolutions. Life was growing more secure and comfortable; manners were softening, while education, science, the arts, and commerce were flourishing. As it colonized the world, Europe had emerged as the wealthiest and most powerful corner of the globe. "Civilized" was a word of longstanding, but the new noun "civilization" served to name a powerful process of change, and to describe its cumulative result.[31]

When President George W. Bush framed 9/11 as an attack on "civilization," dismayed academics churned out learned tracts on the meaning and origin of the word, largely in an attempt to discredit the word itself.[32] You can't have civilization unless someone else is uncivilized, they warned. Worse, they added, reverence for civilization's cherished fruits of safety, abundance, liberty, and democracy can be used to motivate violence on its behalf. And so we are back to *Imagine*. Alert to the dangers of arrogance and war, contemporary academics seem unable to weigh the risks of "civilization" against the dangers of life in a relativist world.

Any society with a lively sense of its own history must necessarily conceive of itself as advancing, declining, or changing in some meaningful way. Short-circuit that process and civilization is cast adrift and defenseless. Maybe that's why the story of civilization was so important to America's Founders.

---

30   Brett Bowden, "The Ideal of Civilization: Its Origin and Socio-Political Character," *Critical Review of International Social and Political Philosophy,*" Vol. 7, No. 1, 2004, p 29.
31   Bruce Mazlish, *Civilization and Its Contents*, (Stanford: Stanford University Press, 2004).
32   Brett Bowden, *The Empire of Civilization: The Evolution of An Imperial Idea*, (Chicago: The University of Chicago Press, 2009), Mazlish, *Civilization and Its Contents*; Roland Robertson, "Civilization," *Theory, Culture & Society*, Vol. 23, No. 2-3, 2006, pp. 421-436.

## Princeton Modern

In 1768, a decade after Jonathan Edwards' death, the Reverend John Witherspoon assumed the presidency of Princeton. Famed as James Madison's mentor and as the only clergyman to sign the Declaration of Independence, Witherspoon is also notable for having introduced the very latest historical and political thought to Princeton.

Lawrence Levine's account of American higher education in the 18th and 19th centuries is a bit of a caricature. It's true that the classical curriculum dominated that era, along with memorization, note-taking, and "recitations" (classroom responses to instructors' questions about assigned readings). Yet Princeton had long experimented with novel subjects and teaching methods.[33] Debates and original compositions were required in James Madison's oratory classes, for which knowledge of history and of then modern authors like Milton, Shakespeare, and Addison was encouraged.[34] Witherspoon himself taught moral philosophy (a combination of ethics, social thought, and current events), and Princeton had introduced chronology (history) shortly before Witherspoon's arrival.[35]

Witherspoon's lectures proselytized for something like a "Great Books" approach. He assured students they could gain an even clearer idea of the ancients from poets like Homer and Horace directly than from historians. Other faculty encouraged students to seek models of virtue, selflessness, and intellect in the classics.[36]

Pre-Revolutionary Princeton taught Western Civilization as well. Witherspoon's practice was to recommend various texts for study in conjunction with his moral philosophy lectures. Montesquieu was featured, as was one of the leading tracts of the then-burgeoning Scottish Enlightenment, Adam Ferguson's 1767 *Essay on the History of Civil Society*.[37] This was the first known English-language publication to use the word "civilization."[38]

The *Essay on the History of Civil Society* is known for its "stage theory." Ferguson saw every human society passing through stages from

---

33 Ralph Ketcham, *James Madison: A Biography*, (New York: Macmillan, 1971), pp. 29-30, 42.
34 David W. Robson, *Educating Republicans: The College in the Era of the American Revolution, 1750-1800*, (Westport, Connecticut: Greenwood Press), pp. 60-61.
35 Ibid., p. 60.
36 Ibid., p. 63.
37 Adam Ferguson, *An Essay on the History of Civil* Society, ed., Fania Oz-Salzberger, (Cambridge: Cambridge University Press, 1995); Ketcham, *James Madison*, 43-45; Robson, *Educating Republicans*, pp. 65-66.
38 Bowden, "The Ideal of Civilization," p. 33.

"savage" to "barbarous" to "polished," and so would equate and discuss, say, the "barbaric" tribes that conquered Rome alongside America's Indians.[39]

Yet Ferguson also tells the story of Europe's unparalleled civilizational development: how it drew its art, science, and law from Greece and Rome, synthesized those with the practices of the "rude" but vigorous Germanic "barbarians," and developed over time into a commercial society that was free, prosperous, militarily powerful, and stabilized by balance-of-power politics within a modern state system.

While Ferguson lauded Europe's progress, he was haunted by the prospect of civilizational decline.[40] He worried that the mechanical luxuries of commercial society along with the rise of professional armies would sap the virtue, discipline, independence, and hardihood of ordinary citizens. Despite its retrograde character in a world of increasingly sophisticated military professionalism, Ferguson believed in the continuing importance of a citizen militia.[41] America's Founders took note.

Absent military service, Ferguson worried that the public would lose the will and capacity to defend themselves against merciless adversaries who rejected the rules of civilized warfare, or to stand against either an internal tyrant or a military coup. Ferguson admired the barbarian toughness of Europe's Germanic ancestors and worried that Britain faced degeneration, decline, and the fate of Rome. No doubt Witherspoon's Ferguson readings informed a student commencement address of 1775 on "The Growth and Decline of Empires," a shot across Britain's bow in the run-up to the Revolution.[42]

Yet it was another history that became America's first great Western Civilization textbook of the 18th and 19th centuries. In 1769, William Robertson, a leader of the Church of Scotland and Principal of the University of Edinburgh, wrote a biography of the Holy Roman Emperor, Charles V. It was Robertson's lengthy introduction to that work that gained fame as the first great narrative account of the development of European civilization: *A View of the Progress of Society in Europe, from the subversion of the Roman Empire to the beginning of the sixteenth century.*[43]

---

39  Lisa Hill, "Adam Ferguson and the Paradox of Progress and Decline," *History of Political Thought*, Vol. XVIII, No. 4, Winter 1997, pp. 677-706.
40  Ibid., pp. 681-683.
41  Bruce Buchan, "Enlightened Histories: Civilization, War and the Scottish Enlightenment," *The European Legacy*, Vol. 10, No. 2, pp. 177-178, 183-187.
42  Robson, *Educating Republicans*, p. 69.
43  William Robertson, *A View of the Progress of Society in Europe, from the subversion of the Roman Empire*

# Robertson's Lost Book

Robertson was hailed in his day as an Enlightenment historian on a par with David Hume and Edward Gibbon.[44] The grand vision of his *View of the Progress of Society in Europe* supplied the background for more specialized European histories well into the 19th century.[45] Yet, notwithstanding a modest revival of scholarly interest in Robertson in the 1990s, this work—which did so much to shape the consciousness of the West—has been virtually forgotten.

Robertson's history of Europe was an immediate sensation in the American colonies, which were in the grip of a pre-Revolutionary fascination with history.[46] Ben Franklin later said that the popular use of libraries in those years had "made the common tradesmen and farmers as intelligent as most gentlemen from other countries."[47] This popular knowledge of history played an important role in inspiring America's defense of its inherited liberties. Popular histories were typically either translated digests of the ancients or accounts of the development of English liberty.[48] The colonists absorbed these histories on the understanding that America was the last great outpost of British freedom and virtue at a time when the mother country itself was beset by luxury and corruption. America came to see themselves as torchbearers of British liberty, perhaps even capable of inspiring a renewal of freedom and virtue in Britain itself.[49] Once again, American exceptionalism took shape against the background of a shared European civilizational story.

Robertson's history of Europe held that Rome would sooner or later have collapsed of its own moral decadence, whether the Goths had invaded or not. This fascinated revolutionaries like Samuel Adams

---

to the beginning of the sixteenth century, (London: W. W. Strahan, 1769), Electronic Library of Historiography, http://www.eliohs.unifi.it/testi/700/robertson/; Stewart J. Brown, "Introduction," in Stewart J. Brown, ed., *William Robertson and the Expansion of Empire*, (Cambridge: Cambridge University Press, 1997), pp. 1-6; Karen O'Brien, "Robertson's Place in the Development of Eighteenth Century Narrative History," in Brown, ed., *William Robertson*, pp. 74-91; Karen O'Brien, *Narratives of Enlightenment: Cosmopolitan History from Voltaire to Gibbon*, (Cambridge: Cambridge University Press, 1997), pp. 129-141; Nicholas Phillipson, "Providence and Progress: An Introduction to the Historical Thought of William Robertson," in Brown, ed., *William Robertson*, pp. 55-73; J. G. A. Pocock, *Barbarism and Religion, Volume Two: Narratives of Civil Government*, (Cambridge: Cambridge University Press, 1999), pp. 258-308; Richard B. Sher, "Charles V and the Book Trade: An Episode in Enlightenment Print Culture," in Brown ed., *William Robertson*, pp. 164-195.

44 Brown, "Introduction," p. 1; Phillipson, "Providence and Progress," p. 55.
45 O'Brien, "Robertson's Place".
46 Trevor Colbourn, *The Lamp of Experience: Whig History and the Intellectual Origins of the American Revolution*, (Indianapolis: Liberty Fund, 1998), available online at http://oll.libertyfund.org/titles/colbourn-the-lamp-of-experience; Sher, "*Charles V.*"
47 Colbourn, "*The Lamp of Experience*," Chapter I, Section III.
48 Ibid., Chapter II, Section I.
49 Ibid., Chapter IX, Section I.

who quoted Robertson enthusiastically, comparing the modern British to the superannuated Romans.[50] Yet Tories and Patriots purchased Robertson's history in equal numbers.[51] So the link between war and America's sense of continuity with Europe's history is more complex than Allardyce would have it. Under the right circumstances, European history has helped precipitate a break with the Continent, as well as a renewed alliance.

Robertson's *View of the Progress of Society in Europe* blended a sophisticated, almost sociological account of European civilization with a broad narrative history, an unprecedented combination at the time. Consider Robertson's account of the Crusades.[52] Voltaire, whose 1756 *Essay on the Manners and Spirit of Nations* was comparable in some ways to Robertson's *View*, largely dismisses the Crusades as superstitious barbarism. Robertson sees waste and folly in that adventure as well. Yet he focuses less on the wisdom of the Crusades than on their social effects.

The Crusades, explains Robertson, stimulated commerce and the growth of towns, while extending the royal jurisdiction. That set up a power struggle between kings and barons, in which both sought to ally with towns by extending their liberties. So the history of Europe is a history of liberty—the continent's unique civilizational marker. Yet liberty's development stems as much from the unintended consequences of self-interested power-plays as from conscious political struggle. Today we take this sort of analysis for granted, yet it was a stunning innovation at the time.

Setting aside Voltaire's bitter excoriation of medieval Christianity, Robertson explored the Church's role in preserving and promoting Roman law, and in generating the intellectual preconditions for the emergence of modern commercial Europe.[53] In short, Robertson replaced Voltaire's anti-religious venom with dispassionate cultural analysis.

While Robertson was alive to the influence of unintended consequences in history, he by no means abandoned faith in the power of conscious moral choice. Unlike other Scottish Enlightenment thinkers, Robertson persistently ranked the pursuit of liberty and the desire for justice as independent historical forces.[54] For Robertson, the quest for

---

50   Ibid., Chapter IV, Section III.
51   Sher, "*Charles V*," p. 191.
52   Pocock, *Barbarism and Religion*, pp. 281-282.
53   Ibid., p. 204.
54   O'Brien, *Narratives of Enlightenment*, pp. 129-141.

"the unalienable rights of humanity" was both an ethical choice and a driver of Europe's story. Divine Providence, as well, retained a role in Robertson's vision.[55]

This balanced and moderate approach to history perfectly suited the American temperament. Rejecting the philosophical skepticism and anti-religious bent of more radical Enlightenment thinkers; Robertson nonetheless acknowledged limits on human agency. We act as free moral agents, yet do so within a political and economic system whose emergence from the feudal background no one foresaw or controlled.

For Robertson, the moral choice most essential to the survival of a free and civilized Europe was the decision to forswear the pursuit of universal empire. Robertson's *History of the Reign of the Emperor Charles V* taught the dangers of the quest for continental hegemony. Britain's king may have tyrannized America, yet his behavior vis-à-vis Europe as a whole was different. Robertson dedicated his biography of Charles V to King George III and honored him for restraint in victory after the Seven Years (or our French and Indian) War. Like Emperor Charles V, or France's Louis XIV, Great Britain's George III could have disrupted the balance of forces in Europe by capitalizing too aggressively on his military victory. Instead King George held back, thereby ensuring Europe's peaceful and free development.[56]

The essence of civilized Europe, for Robertson, was its balance of power. Imperceptibly and unintentionally, the relative chaos of the feudal era had given way to a monarchical state system. Monopolization of force by the state had put an end to religious wars. And paradoxically, the heightened lethality of military technology in the hands of state-controlled professional armies had actually reduced the level of conflict, thereby encouraging commerce, liberty, a softening of manners, and the growth of knowledge.[57]

Yet peace, prosperity, liberty, and the cultural efflorescence they produced all depended upon calculated restraint within a balance-of-power system. In practice, Europe had become a kind of informal confederacy of nations—a civilization bound by a shared system of manners, notwithstanding its periodic internecine wars.[58] Only the pursuit of total continental (and world) domination could disrupt the system, thereby sending civilization into a tailspin.

---

55 Phillipson, "Providence and Progress."
56 Pocock, *Barbarism and Religion*, pp. 276-277.
57 Buchan, "Enlightened Histories," pp. 177-178, 180-181.
58 O'Brien, "Robertson's Place," pp. 75-76; Pocock, *Barbarism and Religion*, p. 2.

# Harvard's Lost Curriculum

Although it hasn't been properly appreciated, Robertson, Montesquieu, and Ferguson, the key early accounts of Western Civilization, all held an important place in Harvard's late-18th century curriculum. Levine misses this because like most scholars of early American education, he focuses on the formal curriculum alone. Yet an unpublished but instructive 1990 doctoral dissertation on Harvard's early curriculum by Thomas Jay Siegel highlights an alternative approach.[59]

Siegel is arguably the first student of early Harvard to give due attention to what he calls the "informal curriculum." Harvard in the 18th century was a provincial university unable to afford the kind of specialized faculty increasingly common in England and Scotland (specialized historians like Robertson, for example).[60] As the Enlightenment burgeoned, Harvard's faculty found it difficult even to assess the growing number of new works, much less incorporate them into the curriculum.[61]

The initial response to this was the growth of student societies dedicated to training in oratory.[62] Groups like the "Speaking Society" read and debated the exciting new work from abroad. By 1773, the college finally stepped in and created a list of books approved for "common use" by students.[63] By this time, Harvard's library had grown into the premiere repository of books in North America.[64] Meanwhile, memorization and recitation were now focused on the mastery of introductory texts during the first two years.[65] Juniors and seniors, in contrast, were increasingly referred by faculty to library work guided by the "common use" list. As Siegel puts it, Harvard's common use list turned what had theretofore been informal study by the student societies into "an integral part of the formal instruction."[66] This was going on at Princeton as well, as when Witherspoon supplemented his moral philosophy lectures with recommended library consultation of Montesquieu and Ferguson.

Robertson, Montesquieu, and Ferguson were all on Harvard's common use list of 1773 and were very heavily borrowed in the years

---

59 Thomas Jay Siegel, "Governance and Curriculum at Harvard College in the 18th Century," Ph.D. thesis dissertation, Harvard University, 1990.
60 Ibid., pp. 231, 254-255.
61 Ibid., p. 274.
62 Ibid., pp. 300-310.
63 Ibid., pp. 321-322.
64 Ibid., p. 318.
65 Ibid., pp. 264-269.
66 Ibid., pp. 274-331, especially pp. 275, 295-297.

leading up to the Revolution.[67] In fact, Robertson's *Charles V* (with its introductory *View of the Progress of Society in Europe*) was the library book most widely borrowed by Harvard students from 1773-1776.[68] Robertson's popularity was likely fueled by a combination of faculty recommendations, student societies, and individual interest. It appears that on the eve of the Revolution, Harvard students were studying Western Civ. In fact, it seems to have been the most popular subject.

More broadly, students in 1775 took history books out of the library more often than any other subject category, amounting to nearly half of all the books borrowed that year.[69] Thus, as Siegel points out, the common reading list effectively incorporated history into the curriculum well before Harvard could afford to hire specialists in the subject. Once you understand the institutionalization of the "informal curriculum" at Harvard, Levine's portrait of early American education sans history falls apart.

History at Harvard in the 18th century was regularly studied with generalist tutors on Saturday afternoons.[70] Textbooks changed over time, but in addition to treatments of the ancients they included histories of Europe, Asia, and Africa. By the end of the century, memorization and recitation of these introductory survey texts in the first two years had become preparation for library work with readings like Robertson, Montesquieu, and Ferguson in the final two years.[71]

In effect, the formal history textbooks served as background for Montesquieu's comparative treatment of world civilizations, with his focus on the West's distinctive character. Finally, around 1783 Montesquieu was incorporated into Harvard's formal curriculum under the novel heading of Politics, to be read under supervision of the Ethics tutor.[72] Robertson remained significant as an approved library text, and in time, as we'll see, would be taken into the official curriculum as well.

---

67  The Common Use list of 1773 can be obtained from Harvard University Archives, Documentary history of the library, 1773-1879; Catalogue Librorum in Bibliotheca Cantabrigiensi Selectus, 178-et seq. HUF 523.6.73, Box 1, Folder 2.
68  Robson, *Educating Republicans*, 87-88; Mark Olsen and Louis-Georges Harvey, "Reading in Revolutionary Times: Book Borrowing from the Harvard College Library, 1773-1782," *Harvard Library Bulletin*, New Series Vol. 4, 1993, pp. 57-72.
69  Siegel, "Governance and Curriculum at Harvard," pp. 319-20, 463
70  Herbert Baxter Adams, *The Study of History in American Colleges and Universities*, (Washington: Government Printing Office, 1887), pp. 14-17.
71  Siegel, "Governance and Curriculum at Harvard," pp. 414, 454-464.
72  Ibid., p. 416.

# Robertson and the Founders

Robertson's penetrating account of the course of European civilization had a significant impact on the Founding generation that is only beginning to be appreciated. In 2013, historian Darren Staloff argued that Robertson's history had profoundly shaped the later philosophy of John Adams.[73] In his early writings, Adams favored a schematically "whiggish" history of Europe in which a despotic "absolute monarchy" had been gradually eroded since the classical era by the spread of education and the love of liberty. Adams was taken aback by Robertson's revelation that strong monarchies were actually late developments and had inadvertently advanced the cause of liberty via self-interested struggle with feudal barons. Robertson's vision of liberty flourishing in an atmosphere of balanced factional and international competition led Adams to rethink his understanding of the Constitution and the presidency.

James Madison had already defended the Constitution in Federalist 10 as an instrument that would preserve liberty by managing balanced factions both within formal governmental structures and in society at large. Conceivably, Madison may have been influenced in this by early readings of Ferguson and Robertson. What we know for certain is that Madison's unfinished and little-known "Notes on Government" manuscript (interpreted and made available to the public for the first time in 2015 by Villanova's Colleen Sheehan) shows him to have been engaged in a dialogue with Adams in the 1790s on the issue of competing factional interest groups.[74] Like Adams, we know that Madison drew heavily on Robertson and other Scottish Enlightenment historians in this post-Federalist Papers work. (Again, Madison had probably studied these historians at Princeton under Witherspoon).

So the debate between Adams' Federalists and Madison's Democrat-Republicans was based on premises that Robertson's popular history had helped to spread. The core idea was that liberty depends upon a balance between multiple cultural and political power centers, an idea that Robertson and the Scotts took from Montesquieu and used to develop a grand narrative of Europe's history.

---

73  Darren Staloff, "John Adams and Enlightenment," in David Waldstreicher, ed., *A Companion to John Adams and John Quincy Adams*, (Chichester, West Sussex: Wiley-Blackwell, 2013), pp. 36-59.

74  Colleen Sheehan, *The Mind of James Madison: The Legacy of Classical Republicanism*, (Cambridge, Cambridge University Press, 2015).

For Jefferson's views on the teaching of history, we have a letter of October 25, 1825 laying out his suggested curriculum for the newly founded University of Virginia.[75] In addition to a substantial study of ancient Greek and Roman history, Jefferson recommends extended readings on modern French and British history. He follows with an ample reading list for "modern Continental history," prominently including both Voltaire's *Spirit and Manners of the Nations* and Robertson's *Charles V* (with its *View of the Progress of Society in Europe*).

This means Levine's claim that Adams and Jefferson would have objected to the teaching of European history could hardly be more mistaken. Adams was actually Robertson's chief exponent in North America, while Jefferson installed Robertson and other readings in Western Civilization at the University of Virginia almost 90 years before World War I began.

With a little digging, Levine could have unearthed Jefferson's actual views on the teaching of "modern" (i.e. post-ancient) European history. Yet Levine's broader portrayal of the early American college curriculum as the work of retrograde pedants is entirely consistent with the scholarship of his day.

# A War for the West

Fortunately, recent work has upended that view, particularly Stanford historian Caroline Winterer's 2002 book, *The Culture of Classicism*.[76] Winterer shows that around 1820, the focus on classical grammar and memorization in the college curriculum gave way to more flexible teaching methods, to an interest in ancient Greek democracy and its cultural implications, and to the emergence of an attitude toward the classical canon that endures to this day. Or, to amend Winterer, we might say that the curricular approach pioneered by Witherspoon at Princeton fifty years before was recovered and advanced more widely at American colleges in the 1820s.

The new approach to the ancients had a double character. On one hand, the Greek and Roman world was lauded as the birthplace of the civilization that helped fashion later European and American life, above

---

75  Herbert Baxter Adams, *Thomas Jefferson and the University of Virginia*, (Washington: Government Printing Office, 1888), pp. 140-142.
76  Winterer, *Culture of Classicism*.

all our democracy, literature, and art. On the other hand, the ancients were held out as a counter-model to the materialism and depraved tastes of modern times. A similar duality shaped Allan Bloom's *Closing of the American Mind* 150 years later.

This period even featured a war in defense of Western civilization. The modern Greek War of Independence from the Ottoman Turks (1821-29) drew volunteers and wide public support throughout the West, very much including American college campuses, where the classical Greeks were increasingly presented as progenitors of Europe's democratic civilization.[77] The pattern fits Allardyce's treatment of World War I, yet by his lights should not have emerged at such an early date.

Particularly during the war's early years, public support for the Greek Revolution generally ran counter to state interests since the Western powers were wary of provoking the Ottomans or destabilizing the Concert of Europe.[78] In the United States, in line with America's traditional policy of avoiding European entanglements, President James Monroe and Secretary of State John Quincy Adams opposed intervention in Greece.[79] This was particularly so since Monroe was about to promulgate what would soon become known as the Monroe Doctrine, a declaration designed to discourage European intervention in the Western hemisphere. So backing for Greece was not statist propaganda but a spontaneous expression of public support for liberty in the birthplace of Western democracy. In contrast to Allardyce and Levine on the link between civilization and war propaganda, this suggests that government-sponsored Western Civilization courses during World War I were likely drawing upon and amplifying a pre-existing set of popular attitudes toward Europe.

The influential Harvard classicist Cornelius Conway Felton, a defender of modern Greece and its struggles for independence, summarized decades of earlier academic work in a popular series of lectures in the early 1850s. These widely read lectures were published and republished in the 1860s and beyond as *Greece Ancient and Modern*.[80] There Felton speaks of the defense and development of "European

---

77  Ibid., 63-64.
78  Alexis Heraclides and Ada Dialla, "Humanitarian intervention in the long nineteenth century: Setting the precedent," 2015, Manchester Scholarship Online: http://manchester.universitypressscholarship.com/view/10.7228/manchester/9780719089909.001.0001/upso-9780719089909-chapter-6
79  Angelo Repousis, "'The Cause of the Greeks': Philadelphia and the Greek War for Independence, 1821-1828," *The Pennsylvania Magazine of History and Biography*, Vol. 123, No. 4, (Oct. 1999),, pp. 333-363.
80  Cornelius Conway Felton, *Greece Ancient and Modern: Lectures Delivered Before the Lowell Institute, In Two Volumes*, (Boston: Ticknor and Fields, 1867). For more on Felton, see Winterer, *Culture of Classicism*, pp. 58-98.

civilization" which he contrasts with the "East."[81] Yet it's clear that Felton sees America holding an honored place within "European" civilization. Particularly in the context of conflict with the Ottomans, Felton also refers to "Christendom," the earlier conception of the West.[82] The phrase "Western civilization" emerged in the 1880s and gained currency in the 20th century, apparently in recognition of America's expanded role in the world. In substance, however, what came to be called "Western civilization" after World War I was fully present as an idea in the early 19th century under the very slightly different name of "European civilization."

Felton was an exceptionalist who believed that America's Constitutional structure more perfectly embodied and advanced the principles of democracy first discovered in ancient Greece than, say, France's then-troubled and unstable political system.[83] This is how exceptionalism was advanced: not in place of the vision of a shared civilizational history, but by means of it.

## Guizot's Great Book

Just as Felton and others were pushing aside the focus on Greek and Latin grammar and memorization in favor of a civilizational reading of the ancient classics, American college students encountered an extraordinary, if now largely forgotten, treatment of Europe's past: Francois Guizot's *The History of Civilization in Europe*. Guizot's lectures on European history would soon become, alongside Robertson's *Progress of Society in Europe*, one of the greatest 19th-century college textbooks on Western Civilization.

Oxford political philosopher Larry Siedentop, who has sought with only limited success to spark a revival of interest in Guizot, calls this lecture series "the most intelligent general history of Europe ever written."[84] Contemporary historians appear to have forgotten not only Guizot's genius and the lessons he imparts, but his impact on American

---

81  Felton, *Greece Ancient and Modern*, Vol. II, pp. 3, 253, 264, 271, 353, 361, 376.
82  Ibid., pp. 264, 384, 411.
83  Ibid., pp. 251-252.
84  Francois Guizot, *The History of Civilization in Europe*, translated by William Hazlitt (1846), edited with an introduction by Larry Siedentop, (London: Penguin Books, 1997), p. vii. Note that references to Guizot below are made to two different editions of his *History of Civilization in Europe*: one edition published ca. 1910, and one edition published in 1997 and introduced by Larry Siedentop. These editions were consulted at different times and are cited separately because the pagination may not correspond. Citations to Guizot's text are from the ca. 1900 edition. Citations to Siedentop's Introduction are to the 1997 edition.

higher education during the 19th century. Yet Guizot lives on through the indelible marks he left on John Stuart Mill, Alexis de Tocqueville, and Karl Marx, the leading political thinkers of that era.[85]

The lectures collected as Guizot's *The History of Civilization in Europe*, were delivered in 1828 under dramatic circumstances. France in the 1820s was ruled by an "ultra-royalist" government that hoped to restore the aristocracy that had controlled France prior to the Revolution. Guizot, a leading inspiration for the partisans of liberal democracy, resisted the ultra-royalists by delivering public lectures on the history of representative government in Europe. The ultra-royalists struck back by suspending university lectures. That ban held until the government fell in 1827, after which Guizot thrilled the democrats of Paris with his series of lectures on European civilization.[86]

Guizot's willingness to speak of progress or stasis in society, and to favorably (and sometimes unfavorably) compare the West with the civilizations of Asia, puts him sharply at odds with today's multiculturalist historians. Guizot holds stable liberal democracy (precisely what France did not then have) as the "final aim of all society," and Europe's imperfect but relative progress toward stable liberal democracy was the ground of his belief in the West's superiority.[87]

Have we truly rejected this belief in the superiority of democracy, or simply driven it underground for fear of appearing intolerant? A case could be made for the moral equivalence of liberal democracy, Middle Eastern tribalism, and the Indian caste system. Yet such relativism would tend to de-legitimize modern democracy (and all social forms), and would also point to challenges of immigration and assimilation that few multiculturalists want to acknowledge or tackle.

Multiculturalism is tough to pin down on such issues since it functions less as a coherent philosophy than a system of contradictory intellectual taboos. Cultures are treated as mild variations on pan-human themes or as profoundly incommensurate, depending on the needs of the moment and the interests at play. Culture now means whatever it has to mean in order to prevent a judgment of relative cultural merit from being made.

As a result, our impulse toward cultural superiority is now directed against the West's own past, rather than other societies. Ironically,

---

85  Ibid., pp. vii-xxxvii.
86  Ibid.
87  François Guizot, *The History of Civilization in Europe*, (New York: A. L. Burt, ca. 1900), Fourteenth Lecture, p. 301.

then, through their very rejection of the Western past, the partisans of cultural relativism recapitulate the traditional Western belief in progress. Paradoxically, they affirm the superiority of a relativist present to our supposedly benighted non-relativist past. Yet this conception of progress is not only far less coherent than Guizot's; it is also less profound.

Bitter as our modern quarrels over America's past can sometimes be, 19th century France faced the more daunting challenge. Ultraroyalists and liberals quarreled over the historical merits of feudalism and of the royalist Catholic Church, as if the very existence of democracy depended on it (as in fact it did). The histories of Christianity and feudalism were wholly condemned or affirmed by the warring camps. Yet by taking a civilizational perspective, Guizot found the road to reconciliation.

Guizot was able to show how a long and winding path led from the Christian principle of the equality of worshipers before God to the revolutionary principles of 1789. Likewise, he showed how the structure of the feudal family had ultimately given birth to the modern regard for individual freedom.[88] Guizot freely condemned the abuses of the past, as, for example, the persecution of heretics. Yet he insisted that the history of formative institutions cannot be radically vitiated by the harm they have sometimes done, since "there is in all things a mixture of good and evil."[89] We could learn much from Guizot today.

Guizot bases his judgement that Europe is unique on its traditions of equal liberty and democracy. His core idea is that democratic development depended crucially on the existence in Europe of multiple and competing centers of cultural and political power, each struggling for dominance yet none able to gain full control. The church, royalty, the feudal aristocracy, and the middle class in Europe's growing cities struggled continually, without final resolution. In the space between them, so to speak, liberty was nurtured and grew. Each competing center of cultural and political power was forced to give an account of its views to the other, and to accept the principle of coexistence. Thus did the cause of liberty advance.[90]

This vision was central to Guizot's comparison of "the West and the rest." Nearly two centuries before Bernard Lewis argued that the failure

---

88  Guizot, *History of Civilization in Europe* (Siedentop introduction), p. xxvii.
89  Guizot, *History of Civilization in Europe* (ca. 1900 edition), Fifth Lecture, p. 114.
90  Guizot, *History of Civilization in Europe* (Siedentop introduction), pp. vii-xxxvii.

to separate religion and the state serves as a barrier to modernization in the Muslim Middle East, for example, Guizot made precisely the same point.[91] The relative differentiation of religion and state was, for Guizot, only one example of the West's characteristically divided and mutually struggling centers of cultural and political power.[92]

In effect, Guizot extended Robertson's argument about the necessary balance of state power and the dangers of universal empire into the cultural realm. It was the failure of the theocratic, monarchic, aristocratic, or even pure democratic principles to gain unchallenged empire over the others that ultimately guaranteed Europe's progress and freedom. Even pure democracy, unchecked, could be abused, as it had been during the excesses of the French Revolution. (Guizot's moderate view of democracy and of the need for checks and balances is thoroughly compatible with America's Constitutional system.)

The 19th century belief in historical progress is often criticized as self-regarding, since historians have generally placed their own societies at the apex of social evolution. Yet while Guizot insisted, justifiably, on France's leading role on the continent, he placed England rather than France at the head of European civilization. More than any other part of Europe, Guizot maintained that England had succeeded in creating multiple and simultaneous centers of cultural and political power, particularly given the importance of local institutions in that country. As a result, England had moved further toward stable liberal democracy than any other European power.[93] Like Montesquieu, Guizot was an "English exceptionalist."

## Guizot's Long Reach

Recent work by British intellectual historian Georgios Varouxakis establishes that Guizot's *The History of Civilization in Europe* had a transformative effect on John Stuart Mill, who tirelessly promoted Guizot's lectures in the English-speaking world.[94] Early in his career, Mill had

---

91  Bernard Lewis, *What Went Wrong: Western Impact and Middle Eastern Response*, (New York: Oxford University Press, 2002); Guizot, *History of Civilization in Europe* (ca. 1900 edition), Third Lecture, p. 63.
92  To cite the relative independence of religion and state in the West is not to endorse any specific contemporary call for "separation of church and state." Arguably, some contemporary advocates of a thoroughgoing separation between church and state are themselves breaking with traditional practice in both America and the West.
93  Guizot, *History of Civilization in Europe* (ca. 1900 edition), Fourteenth Lecture, pp. 298-301.
94  Georgios Varouxakis, "Guizot's Historical Works and J.S. Mill's Reception of Tocqueville," *History of Political Thought*, Vol. XX, No. 2. Summer 1999, pp.292-312.

accepted the (pre-Marxist) "utopian socialist" view that society ought to be led by the educated classes, what he called the "clerisy." Yet after reading Guizot's account of liberty's dependence upon multiple and competing power centers, Mill turned against the idea of rule by an intellectual elite. Mill's classic defense of free thought and discussion in *On Liberty* was built around his conviction, inspired by Guizot, that the further progress of liberty depended upon the clash of competing perspectives.

Guizot had written of Europe's historical struggle among royalty, church, aristocracy, and the middle classes. In Mill's view, however, the threat of domination by a single class lived on in a different form in his Victorian Age. In modern Europe, Mill came to believe, the looming danger was rule by a clerisy—an educated elite, while for America (this being the Jacksonian era) Mill feared the unchallenged domination of democratic populism. For Mill, the West's continued freedom and progress depended upon the continued and unresolved clash of these interests and perspectives within a given country.

Alexis de Tocqueville, who's great study of American democracy virtually "invented" the analytical concept of American exceptionalism (although the *phenomenon* had been of long standing), took his central inspiration from Guizot's Paris lectures on European civilization.[95] Tocqueville had attended those lectures and later studied them with care.[96] Guizot's contrast between England's localizing and democratic tendencies and France's more centralized but less stable democracy drew Tocqueville's attention. Guizot's related praise of America's federalist system as a particularly advanced form of democratic localism then pushed Tocqueville to look to America for a solution to France's enervating bureaucratic centralization.

Guizot's account of the rise and insurrection of the modern commercial middle classes against an oppressive feudal aristocracy also became the inspiration for Marx's theory of historical materialism.[97] Marx modeled his vision of a proletarian revolution on Guizot's account of the earlier conflict between the nobility and the bourgeoisie. Characteristically, Marx both affirmed and inverted the wisdom of his source of inspiration. Whereas Guizot saw an unresolved struggle of

---

95  Alexis de Tocqueville, *Democracy in America*, Translated by George Lawrence, ed. by J. P. Mayer and Max Lerner, (New York: Harper & Row, 1966).
96  Guizot, *History of Civilization in Europe* (Siedentop introduction), pp. xxx-xxxii.
97  Ibid., pp. xxx-xxxv.

competing social power centers as the guarantor of liberty, Marx looked to a fully victorious dictatorship of the proletariat to put an end to the sham freedom and democracy of the bourgeoisie.

Through his influence on Marx, Guizot can rightly be seen as a progenitor of modern sociology. Yet the spirit of Guizot's work was closer to Robertson's "philosophical history" than to modern social science. Guizot's account of the rise of the middle classes was designed to prove to the ultra-royalists that feudalism had long-since been irrevocably transformed, and therefore could never be simply restored. Yet while Guizot, like Robertson, believed that social structure and the unintended course of history set limits on political choice, he also affirmed, in contrast to modern social determinists, the power of free will as a shaper of history within those broader constraints.

Neither Allardyce nor Levine has anything to say about Robertson's *Progress of Society in Europe* or Guizot's *History of Civilization in Europe*, although both these books are general accounts of Western history of the highest intellectual order that were profoundly influential college textbooks throughout much of the 19th century. This act of forgetting would have been impossible had contemporary historians consulted a readily available 1887 work by one of America's first professional historians, Herbert Baxter Adams: *The Study of History in American Colleges and Universities*.[98]

This modest empirical study, prepared by Adams at the request of what was then the Bureau of Education in the Department of the Interior, effectively explodes the simplistic and condescending view of early American education favored by Allardyce and Levine. Let's begin with Harvard, since its influence on the direction of American education in the 19th century was unparalleled.

We have seen that in the 18th century, Harvard students had regular time set aside each week for the study of history survey textbooks, supplemented for juniors and seniors by advanced but informal work with the likes of Montesquieu, Ferguson, and Robertson. Eventually, as memorization of survey textbooks was confined to the first two years, Montesquieu was incorporated into the formal curriculum as an advanced text.

Adams explains the next big shift, which came in 1839 when Harvard appointed Jared Sparks, Washington's biographer and the man then widely regarded as America's finest historian, as its first professor of

---

98  Adams, *The Study of History*.

history.[99] Sparks quickly swapped out the uninspired history textbooks required of sophomores in 1820 for a synthetic account of the fall of the Roman Empire and Guizot's *History of Civilization in Europe*. Robertson's *Progress of Society in Europe* was soon added as a sophomore text. Then, from 1840, Harvard Juniors, not previously required to study history, were regularly assigned William Smyth's ambitious *Lectures on Modern History, From the Irruption of the Northern Nations* [i.e. from the fall of Rome] *To the Close of The American Revolution*, in an edition prefaced by Sparks himself.[100] Henry Hallam's *View of the State of Europe During the Middle Ages* was also required of juniors.[101] Meanwhile, Sparks personally taught Harvard's first required course in American history to seniors.

None of this came at the expense of ancient history. Sparks actually expanded the use of English language textbooks on Greek and Roman history, particularly for freshmen. At the same time Cornelius Conway Felton, the Harvard classicist who helped to introduce the civilizational approach to the ancient classics, was pioneering in the use of carefully selected passages (in the original Greek) from Herodotus and Thucydides to teach both language and ancient history.

So from about 1840 to 1870, far from not having been invented yet, as Allardyce and Levine maintain, it would be fair to say that Western Civilization in a recognizably modern sense had colonized the lion's share of what we now call the "humanities" curriculum at Harvard. (The term "humanities" gained currency during the 1880s.)[102] True, daily student recitations remained in use, and this limited the ability of professors and students to explore the material more fully. Yet along with the assignment of intellectually ambitious readings, professorial lectures expanded during this period.[103] A more modern curriculum was clearly taking shape.

---

99  Ibid., pp. 17-18.
100 William Smyth, *Lectures on Modern History, From the Irruption of the Northern Nations To the Close of The American Revolution*, (Cambridge: John Owen, 1841).
101 Henry Hallam, *View of the State of Europe During the Middle Ages*, (New York: W. J. Widdleton, 1866).
102 James Turner, *The Liberal Education of Charles Eliot Norton*, (Baltimore: The Johns Hopkins University Press, 1999), pp. 257, 380.
103 Ibid., p. 46.

# Sparks Fly

Once you know a bit more about Jared Sparks, his expansion of required European studies at Harvard becomes all the more striking. Sparks had met Guizot on an 1828 research trip to Europe, arriving in Paris just as Guizot's lectures on European civilization had become the talk of the city. There Sparks was able to secure Guizot's agreement to issue a French translation of Sparks' edition of Washington's works.[104] So on top of the general interest in the English-speaking world in Guizot's lectures set off by John Stuart Mill (whose work the Boston literati followed closely), Sparks would have had ample direct familiarity with Guizot's account of European civilization.

But it was Sparks' encounter with another famous Frenchman that paints all this in a new light. In 1831, on the trip out of which his classic study of American democracy would emerge, Alexis de Tocqueville arrived in Boston. Tocqueville was immediately struck by the refinement and intellectual accomplishments of Boston's elite. Almost all the women possessed an excellent command of French (and of the latest Paris fashions), while the men had all been to Europe.[105] Tocqueville was quickly introduced to Sparks, who answered inquiries on the character of American democracy with an impromptu lecture on the history and significance of local government in the United States. Tocqueville was so impressed that he asked Sparks to elaborate in a written account, and this document became arguably the chief source for Tocqueville's claim that America's exceptional inclination toward liberty is rooted in the history and structure of its local government.[106]

In short, the man who more than any other taught Tocqueville the meaning of American exceptionalism is the same man who institutionalized the study of Western Civilization at Harvard. Levine's distinction between an exceptionalist 19th century America, turned in on itself and uninterested in Europe, and a post-World War I America anchored in transatlantic ties, is untenable. Americans in the 19th century looked to Europe for inspiration, and for the beginnings of an understanding of who they were, while also believing that America had developed and perfected the career of liberty to an unprecedented degree.

---

104 Herbert Baxter Adams, *The Life and Writings of Jared Sparks*, (Cambridge, Massachusetts: The Riverside Press, 1893), pp. 97-120.
105 George Wilson Pierson, *Tocqueville in America*, (Baltimore: Oxford University Press, 1938 [Johns Hopkins University Press Paperback edition, 1996]), pp. 362-366.
106 Ibid. pp. 366-368, 397-416.

To a considerable extent, even continental thinkers like Guizot and Tocqueville embraced these claims of American uniqueness. Nor was 19th century America's interest in Europe and its history confined to the well-traveled Boston elite.

While the early 19th century saw what was then called "modern" (i.e. post-ancient) history enter the college curriculum through the influence of esteemed figures like Thomas Jefferson and Jared Sparks, pressure on colleges to introduce modern history was also bubbling up from public primary and secondary schools.[107] The private academies that prepared students for college entrance exams in Greek and Latin had little use for history. Yet as public education spread, the 18th century ideal of the "philosophical gentleman" was challenged by a more popular and pragmatic vision of an education focused on modern languages, geography, and history. Reading primers for the early grades ca. 1850 devoted about twenty percent of their space to history. In the same period, high school history textbooks proliferated and state legislatures increasingly mandated history classes. City and state colleges, more directly subject to public pressure than elite private universities, responded to this trend.

Perhaps the most striking example of this is the University of Michigan, which in 1857 hired Andrew Dickson White, an American historian who had received extensive training in Europe.[108] White quickly went about establishing a four-year course on history within the required curriculum. White had freshmen studying ancient, medieval and modern history, sophomores reading Robertson's *Progress of Society in Europe*, juniors mastering Guizot, and a series of lectures by White himself for seniors exploring all of that material more deeply. This was, in effect, a required four-year sequence in Western Civilization. In the 1860s, White became a co-founder and the first president of Cornell University, where he introduced a similar approach.

Although ignored by Allardyce and Levine, the evidence that Guizot's *History of Civilization in Europe* was widely taught at America's colleges and universities throughout much of the 19th century is abundant. Herbert Baxter Adams, who relied not only on in-depth studies of numerous colleges, but on an extensive survey conducted by the U.S. Bureau of Education, concluded that Guizot "has probably been

---

107 George H. Callcott, "History Enters the Schools," *American Quarterly*, Vol. 11, No. 4, Winter, 1959, pp. 470-483.

108 Adams, *The Study of History*, pp. 94-100; 124-135; Ruth Bordin, *Andrew Dickson White: Teacher of History*, (Ann Arbor: University of Michigan, 1958), Michigan Historical Collections Bulletin, No. 8, pp. 11-17.

used more than any other [history] textbook for advanced or senior courses in American colleges."[109] One of Sparks' correspondents wrote in 1851, just twelve years after Sparks had introduced Guizot at Harvard, "Guizot's *History of Civilization* is used in half the colleges of the country."[110] That proportion only grew with time. The University of Pittsburgh, for example, added Guizot's lectures to the required curriculum during the Civil War, where they remained until at least 1891.[111] And Guizot was as popular with the public as with the schools. An 1862 article in America's premiere intellectual journal of the day, the *North American Review*, says Guizot's *History of Civilization in Europe* has "been read as widely as the most popular novel," this in an era during which Levine claims Americans were uninterested in any history but their own.[112] A 1933 study of the development of the American social science curriculum put the period of Guizot's widespread popularity as a college textbook at "more than fifty years." This would stretch from about 1840 through the end of the century.[113]

If you are studying Guizot, you are studying Western civilization. And remember, Guizot was generally assigned to students who had earlier been required to read more conventional narrative accounts of ancient and modern history. Combine this with the fact that language instruction in the Greek and Latin classics was increasingly done with an eye toward historical substance and civilizational continuity, and it's fair to say that virtually the entire humanities curriculum during the bulk of the 19th century amounted to a course in Western Civilization.

## Exceptionalists Prove the Rule

Adams tells us that reading Guizot's lectures "has proved epoch-making in many a student's life."[114] That certainly applies to Andrew Dickson White, who first read Guizot at Yale and was transformed by the experience. And there are other examples of Guizot's influence on 19th century Americans.

---

109  Adams, *The Study of History*, p. 99.
110  Adams, *The Life and Writings of Jared Sparks*, p. 461.
111  Alfred P. James, "The Study of History in the University of Pittsburgh," *Western Pennsylvania Historical Magazine*, Vol. 9, No. 4, Oct. 1926, pp. 232-235.
112  Christian Charles Josias Bunsen, "Leading Theories on the Philosophy of History: Outlines of the Philosophy of Universal History," *The North American Review*, Vol. XCV, 1862, p. 186.
113  L. L. and J. S. Bernard, "A Century of Progress in the Social Sciences," *Social Forces*, Vol. 11, No. 4, May, 1933, p. 490.
114  Adams, *The Study of History*, p. 96.

Lewis Henry Morgan, an American social thinker who influenced Darwin, Marx, and Freud, was set on his path by a course on Guizot at Union College in Schenectady, New York, around 1840.[115] Morgan really did "invent" the modern anthropological study of kinship, and his reconstructions of pre-history based on kinship practices were influential in Europe and America and were taken up in detail by Marx and Freud.

Morgan's conception of modern society, in turn, was deeply indebted to Guizot.[116] In principle, Morgan agreed with Guizot that their shared history put Europe and the United States on a common pathway toward the achievement and perfection of individual liberty. In practice, however, Morgan tended to stress the ways in which the absence of an aristocratic tradition and of Europe's grinding poverty had allowed America to achieve more fully than others a stable liberal democracy. The result was a classically exceptionalist take on America that was nevertheless thoroughly informed by Guizot's understanding of Western social development. Again, the Allardyce-Levine dichotomy between American exceptionalism and interest in the history of European civilization fails to fit the facts.

There was no greater 19th century exponent of patriotism, exceptionalism, and manifest destiny than William McGuffey, author of the most popular American textbook of all time, the *McGuffey Readers*.[117] A 1927 *Saturday Evening Post* piece concluded that the Fourth, Fifth, and Sixth *McGuffey Readers* (the sixth was directed to high schools, colleges, and the general public), "probably exerted a greater influence...upon the morality of the United States than any other books, excepting the Bible."[118] *McGuffey Readers* were filled with history and literature, American and European. And McGuffey himself, a professor of "mental and moral philosophy" at the University of Virginia, assigned Guizot, supplemented by readings from Adam Ferguson, for his college courses through the 1840s and 50s.[119] So this immensely influential paragon of

---

115   Daniel Noah Moses, *Promise of Progress: The Life and Work of Lewis Henry Morgan*, (Columbia, Missouri: The University of Missouri Press, 2009), p. 15.
116   Ibid., pp. 15, 16, 35, 126-128.
117   Quentin R. Skrabec, Jr., *William McGuffey: Mentor to American Industry*, (New York, Algora Publishing, 2009).
118   Ibid., p. 232.
119   J. Graham Morgan, "Preparation for the Advent: The Establishment of Sociology as a Discipline in American Universities in the Late Nineteenth Century," *Minerva*, Vol. 20, No. 1/2, March 1982, p. 27.

American exceptionalism was also a teacher and acolyte of Guizot (and Ferguson). Yet the influence of Guizot on 19th century Americans has been almost entirely forgotten.

## A Thesis Radicalized

Before we examine the conception of Western civilization in the final decades of the 19th century, let's briefly review and reconsider Allardyce's argument and how it's been developed.

The Allardyce thesis has grown more ambitious as scholars have adopted and adapted it. Allardyce himself, at least in passing, draws a distinction between the Western Civilization *course*, which he calls "a characteristically American invention," and the broader Western perception of a "European civilization," which he acknowledges the United States inherited from Europe early on.[120] So at one point, Allardyce appears to be claiming only that the Western civilization *course* was invented during World War I, not the idea of Western civilization itself. Allardyce's argument does not rest there, however.

Allardyce never seriously explores America's early inheritance of the idea of European civilization. More important, the thrust of his analysis contrasts the (allegedly) dominant pre-World War I idea of a frontier-focused and exceptionalist America with the (allegedly) characteristic post-World War I American vision of a shared Western history. By the end of Allardyce's argument, then, the creation of the Western civilization course appears to be the effective advent in America of the idea of Western Civilization itself.

Levine's interest in drawing Allardyce into his argument against proponents of the Western Civilization course leads him to drop even the perfunctory acknowledgement that Americans before World War I felt civilizational ties to Europe. As Levine puts it, "Nineteenth-century Americans did not tend to conceive of themselves as participants in a common Western civilization."[121] The effect of Levine's sharp historical dichotomy is to radicalize the argument, elevating it to a claim that the very idea of Western civilization is largely a late invention coterminous with the Post-World War I course itself.

---

120  Allardyce, "Rise and Fall," p. 699.
121  Levine, *Opening*, p. 60.

This polemical expansion of the Allardyce thesis then culminates in sweeping formulations like Lynn Hunt's recent claim in *Time Magazine* that "'Western civilization' was invented during World War I as a way of explaining to American soldiers why they were going to fight in Europe."[122]

As we've seen, however, America's commitment to the idea of membership in a shared European civilization flourished long before World War I, and comfortably coexisted with classic American exceptionalism from the start. The exceptionalist claim was not that we had no part in a common European civilization, but rather that we were perfecting it.

## Fallacies

Over and above its uses for military recruitment and for the legitimization of America's growing international power, Allardyce points to another impetus for the popularity of Western Civilization courses in the early 20$^{th}$ century. Allardyce argues that the Western Civilization course emerged, in part, as a response to the curricular chaos fomented by an academic revolution that began at Harvard in 1870 and played out on America's college campuses through the 1910s.[123] During these decades the elective system emerged and pushed aside the required classical curriculum. This was also the period when history and other academic disciplines were professionalized along European lines, and the professoriate turned toward an emphasis on specialized research. Allardyce argues that the triumph of the elective system and the consequent loss of common readings produced a craving for the return of "general education."[124] This reactive impulse toward commonality, in combination with the advent of the Great War and America's expanded role in the world, is what Allardyce says led to the "invention" of the Western Civilization course.

To pull this argument off, however, Allardyce has to ignore some critical evidence. When President Charles William Eliot, who introduced the elective system, became president of Harvard in 1869, ancient, medieval, modern, and American history were already being taught

---

122  Rothman, "The Problem with Rep. Steve King's Take."
123  Allardyce, "Rise and Fall," pp. 699-703.
124  Ibid., pp. 703-709.

at the school. Allardyce's argument would fail if those courses were already pervaded by the idea of a shared civilization of the West. Yet Allardyce dismisses Harvard's pre-Eliot history curriculum as the work of a mere amateur, a "dear old gentleman" with no professional training in history.[125]

This "dear old gentleman" was Henry W. Torrey, who was a tutor under Jared Sparks, and who advanced to his own professorship in the years that followed.[126] Had Allardyce or Levine (who also dismisses Torrey as an amateur) inquired, they would have discovered that Torrey taught a Harvard course from 1856 through 1870 in general European history, using Robertson and Guizot among other texts, a bona fide Western Civilization course if there ever was one.[127]

At various points, both Allardyce and Levine confuse the issue of the professionalization of the faculty with an argument about the content of the curriculum. Levine, for example, points out how few history professors taught before about 1870.[128] Yet this misses figures like McGuffey, a professor of "mental and moral philosophy" who regularly assigned Guizot. True, such scholars were not research-based professional historians in the modern sense. Yet even classic mid-20th century Western Civilization courses were largely conducted by junior faculty and teaching assistants, precisely because senior faculty found general education a distraction from their specialized research. In the 19th century, it was often the president of the college who would teach Guizot. General education has always favored generalists.

Allardyce and Levine also miss the fact (highlighted by Winterer) that European-trained scholars and historians began to transform American higher education well before 1870.[129] Many of these European-trained scholars actually favored the civilizational approach, Andrew Dickson White, for example.

In the end, then, both Allardyce and Levine condescend to American higher education prior to its professionalization and secularization in the late 1800s. Neither bothers to inquire in any serious way into the content of the history curriculum prior to the creation of Harvard's

---

125  Ibid., p. 699.
126  Adams, *The Study of History*, pp. 26-30.
127  Ibid.; Levine, *Opening*, p. 41.
128  Ibid., pp. 41-42.
129  Winterer, *Culture of Classicism*, pp. 44-76.

elective system in the 1870s. Levine simply assumes that an educational system "suffused with a religious ethos and purpose," can neither be thoughtful nor innovative.[130] As we have seen, that is wrong.

Allardyce also defines his problem as the "invention" of the Western Civilization *course*.[131] Yet this precludes from the start the possibility that what had been condensed into a single 20<sup>th</sup> century class about Western Civilization may have earlier been spread out across the traditional curriculum, from original language readings in the classics, to separate courses on ancient Greece, ancient Rome, and modern Europe. In other words, by the very framing of his problem as the construction of a single comprehensive course, Allardyce virtually rules out the possibility that Western Civilization might have been taught prior to 1870. In fact, the 20<sup>th</sup> century Western Civilization course was essentially a condensation and concentration of large tracts of the 19<sup>th</sup> century curriculum into a single course. That single class would necessarily have placed great emphasis on civilizational continuity. Yet as we have seen, the notion of civilizational continuity from the ancients to the moderns had emerged well before the modern curriculum did.

In the end, neither the idea nor the teaching of Western Civilization was "invented" during World War I. What really happened in the early 20<sup>th</sup> century was the return of a teaching theme that had dominated the 19<sup>th</sup> century prior to the advent of the elective system in the 1870s.

A thoughtful 1933 article from *Social Forces* by L. L. and J. S. Bernard on the history of the social science curriculum is particularly helpful in this regard.[132] After noting the popularity of Guizot as a textbook during the 19<sup>th</sup> century, and highlighting the civilizational perspective of scholars of the period like Andrew Dickson White, the Bernards remark: "More recently, especially since the great war, there has been something of a return to emphasis upon the history of civilization, both in general historical writing and in the introductory courses in history in the college curricula."[133] So a couple of academic observers who actually lived through the post-World War I efflorescence of the Western Civilization course took it not to be an unprecedented novelty but a return to an earlier perspective.

---

130 Levine, *Opening*, p. 37.
131 Allardyce, "Rise and Fall," pp. 695, 699.
132 Bernard, "A Century of Progress in the Social Sciences," pp. 488-505.
133 Ibid., p. 491.

# Forgotten Figure

Notwithstanding this continuity, can we at least say that the teaching of Western civilization was suspended between 1870 and World War I, the period of the elective system's unchallenged dominance? We cannot. In addition to the fact that it took time for the elective system to reach many schools, even at Harvard, the center of the elective revolution, Western civilization re-emerged as a theme well before World War I. We glean this from Notre Dame historian James Turner's justly praised 1999 study of Charles Eliot Norton, a highly influential figure from Harvard's past.[134] In his biography of Norton, and in a 2000 study (co-authored with Jon H. Roberts) of the college curriculum between the Civil War and World War I, Turner argues that Charles Eliot Norton effectively "invented" the idea of Western civilization in the 1890s.[135]

Although all but forgotten now, Charles Eliot Norton was the most widely known and respected American intellectual of his day. His Fine Arts survey courses were regularly attended by up to a third of Harvard's student body. Because of Norton's prominence, not to mention the cultural impact of his many students, his pedagogical and curricular ideas spread widely.

Norton's survey courses presented the history of Western art, from classical Greece and Rome through modern Europe, in a civilizational setting, with a selection of Great Books including Homer, Dante, and Shakespeare included for context. Norton stressed cultural continuities and chains of influence from ancient times to the present day. Turner's account of Norton's teaching thus constitutes one of the few scholarly challenges to the Allardyce thesis.[136]

Neither Turner's methods nor his aims are particularly deconstructionist. Turner's claim that Norton "invented" Western Civilization is less an attempt to debunk the Western tradition than an argument for Norton's significance. Turner's "invention" claim exaggerates Norton's originality, although clearly Norton's adaptation of the pre-existing Western civilization idea to the modern curriculum was significant. Norton aimed to serve as a counterweight to the narrow specialization and value-free ethos of Harvard's newly specialized and

---

134 Turner, *Liberal Education*.
135 Jon H. Roberts and James Turner, *The Sacred and The Secular University*, (Princeton: Princeton University Press, 2000).
136 Turner, *Liberal Education*, pp. 368-392, 464-465; Roberts and Turner, *The Sacred and The Secular University*, pp. 96-106, 169-170.

professionalized curriculum. His creation of a survey sequence supplemented by a Great Books curriculum in the midst of the elective revolution was a breakthrough. And it all happened well before World War I.

Turner understands that his claims for Norton are at odds with the current scholarly consensus on the intellectual and pedagogical origins of Western Civilization, yet he seems to want to keep his head down. Turner says nothing directly about Allardyce, and buries such limited comments as he ventures on the scholarly controversy in his endnotes. What Turner says is important nonetheless.

Although Charles Eliot Norton was obviously teaching a course on Western Civilization in the 1890s, he did not use precisely that term. Typically, he spoke simply of "our" civilization, meaning the civilization shared by Europeans and Americans.[137] Roberts and Turner point out that the term "Western civilization" was being used unselfconsciously at least as early as 1890.[138] So how much stock should we put in the conventional view that the first curricular appearance of a Wester Civ course followed directly from World War I? According to Roberts and Turner, "If by 'Western civilization course' is meant a course that explicitly uses the word *civilization* in its title and that runs from antiquity to the present, then the conventional view is right, though hardly to the point."[139]

It seems obvious, following Turner, that the substance of the curriculum matters more than a title. Yet the seemingly trivial matter of the course title has taken on untoward significance because so many contemporary historians have lost faith in the reality of continuous cultural traditions, be they national, civilizational, religious or otherwise. From that perspective, such cultural continuity as exists is attributed to the selfish interests of a dominant group, and the goal becomes tracing novel verbal "constructions" of tradition back to the interests of various power-holders. With the energy of contemporary historians increasingly invested in this postmodernist quest, the result resembles a denial of history itself. Continuity is increasingly ignored or discredited, when its very possibility is not denied. For the most part, then, no one has bothered to determine whether functional equivalents of the modern Western Civilization course—or idea—existed in earlier times, even if under slightly different names. Having put forward the

---
137 Turner, *Liberal Education*, p. 384.
138 Roberts and Turner, *The Sacred and The Secular University*, p. 170.
139 Ibid.

politically congenial link between "Western Civ" classes and wartime propaganda, the Allardyce thesis has quickly come to be taken as "too good to check."

Charles Eliot Norton's example undermines the Allardyce thesis in more ways than one. Not only did Norton offer a Western Civilization survey decades before the First World War, his understanding of the relationship between civilization and war nearly turns the Allardyce thesis on its head. Norton was an ardent anti-imperialist who saw his survey course as a way of arresting America's retreat from civilization and its slide into a warlike "barbarism." Perhaps the most visible opponent of America's involvement in the Spanish-American war, Norton's courageous 1898 anti-war address, "True Patriotism" evoked widespread obloquy and abuse. Although forgotten by most, Norton's speech is still occasionally reprinted in anthologies favored by the anti-war left.[140]

Contemporary historians are correct to discern a connection between the idea of civilization and the call for a common defense against its enemies. And certainly the idea of a civilizing mission has been used to justify colonialism, as historians are quick to remind us. Yet these same historians largely neglect the other side of the coin. The idea of civilization implies restraint in war, and lays down a standard of justice by which conflicts can be judged and condemned. Ferguson worried that civilized moderns would lose their fierce independence, yet also valued the restraint of civilized warfare. Likewise, Robertson praised George III for foregoing the pursuit of universal empire. And in 1814, Benjamin Constant, a French liberal theorist and contemporary of Guizot, issued a sweeping condemnation of Napoleon's imperial conquests in the name of the ever-advancing mores of "European civilization."[141]

Norton, a co-founder of the liberal magazine, *The Nation*, stood foursquare in this tradition of civilizational critiques of war. The most important difference between Norton and his modern leftist successors is that Norton was deeply serious about his patriotism, which he based not on a sense of ethnic belonging, but on the universal principles of equality and liberty embodied in America's republican system—and

---

140 Charles Eliot Norton, "True Patriotism: A Speech Delivered at the Men's Club of the Prospect Street Congregational Church in Cambridge, Mass., June 7, 1898," Mises Institute, Mises Daily Articles, April 8, 1999, https://mises.org/library/true-patriotism; Turner, *Liberal Education*, pp. 368-372, 393-397; Jesse Stellato, ed., *Not in Our Name: American Antiwar Speeches, 1846 to the Present*, ( University Park, Penn State University Press, 2012).

141 Benjamin Constant, *Political Writings*, (Cambridge: Cambridge University Press, 1988), pp. 43-168; Jennifer Pitts, *A Turn to Empire: The Rise of Imperial Liberalism in Britain and France*, (Princeton: Princeton University Press, 2005), pp. 173-183.

nurtured over the history of ancient and modern Europe. Ironically, then, this giant of the teaching of Western civilization is a progenitor of a leftist professoriate now largely blind to its own heritage. Indeed postmodern historians increasingly reject the very possibility of an authentic heritage.

If Turner's account of Norton's innovations is compelling, his claim that Norton "invented" Western civilization is untenable. Norton himself attended Harvard in the early 1840s, just as Jared Sparks was infusing both ancient and modern Western history into the curriculum, and Just as Cornelius Felton was beginning to teach the ancient classics from a recognizably modern civilizational perspective. Turner allows that Norton drew at least the germ of his ideas from this earlier background. Yet his attempts to distinguish Norton's achievement from these earlier precedents are unconvincing.

Although Turner understands that Norton was deeply influenced by the Scottish Enlightenment in his youth, he attempts to differentiate Norton's more pessimistic view of history from the Scots'. Yet Ferguson was an ambivalent progressivist, confident of long-term progress yet keenly aware of the dangers of civilizational backsliding, much like Norton.

Turner also seems unaware of the reach of Robertson and Guizot, both at Harvard and beyond. Turner mentions Guizot in passing (and then only for his influence on a Princeton professor), and seeks to distinguish Guizot's notion of civilization as a pan-human phenomenon from Norton's focus on a specifically European civilization. Of course Guizot's famous lectures were precisely on civilization in Europe, which he considered the modern vanguard of the pan-human quest for civilization. So it's tough to distinguish Norton's notion of a shared European civilization from Robertson's, Guizot's, or Felton's; all those views were shaping Harvard long before the 1890s.

Turner also distinguishes the religious focus of mid-19th century moral psychology courses from Norton's more secular "cultural" approach. Yet Robertson and Guizot, while not incompatible with religion, offered a largely secular cultural approach as well. In short, the scholarly amnesia regarding the place of Robertson and Guizot in the 18th and 19th century curriculum has led to a series of spurious assertions about the late invention of a Western civilization that has in fact been studied by college students since before the American Revolution.

Norton's real innovation was combining civilizational strands—ancient, medieval, and modern—that had previously been explored in separate classes, thereby emphasizing their continuity. Yet the notion of continuous influence running from the Greeks through the present was already one of Felton's mid-century themes. And while Guizot began his account at the fall of the Roman Empire, like Norton he stressed the way in which ancient civilization's accomplishments had been passed on to modern Europe. In short, Norton helped rescue and resuscitate the idea of Western civilization. And because the various stages and strands of that civilization were condensed into a single survey course, Norton explored their links more fully than his predecessors. Yet while he may have helped to save Western Civilization for his era, Norton hardly invented it.

## FDR Gets a B

Nor was Norton alone in teaching Western Civilization at Harvard in the 1890s. From 1893 through 1904, famed Harvard historian Archibald Cary Coolidge taught History I, a classic Western Civilization course that enjoyed a celebrated half-century run at Harvard, while serving as a prototype for similar courses across the country. Although Allardyce knows nothing of Norton's Fine Arts version of Western Civ, he understands that Coolidge's History I poses a mortal threat to the claim that Western Civ was created to motivate soldiers to fight the First World War. Although Allardyce strains mightily to deny that Coolidge's course of the 1890s was an authentic version of Western Civ, his argument does not hold up.[142]

Allardyce's treats Coolidge's History I as the stunted predecessor of a full-blown 20$^{th}$ century Western Civ class. Those classes, Allardyce argues, were modeled on Columbia's post-World War I "Contemporary Civilization" course, which itself emerged from years of academic experiments like Coolidge's novelties at Harvard. As Allardyce puts it, "Western Civ did not come into existence fully assembled, nor was it conceived in one swoop at Columbia in 1919."[143] This framing allows Allardyce to present Coolidge's (1890s) History I as an outmoded experimental prototype of Columbia's richer 1919 Contemporary Civ class.

---

142  Allardyce, "Rise and Fall," pp. 700-703.
143  Ibid., p. 699.

And of course that allows Allardyce to argue that Western Civ must be considered a direct product of Columbia's War Issues course (the immediate predecessor of Columbia's 1919 course in Contemporary Civilization) for soldiers during the First World War.[144]

To support this claim, Allardyce offers a misleading account of Coolidge's course of the 1890s. As Allardyce presents it, Coolidge was hamstrung by a preoccupation with historical fact: "To [Coolidge], freshman history was factual history, and quizzes, map drills, and recitations on lectures and textbooks were the order of the day in section work."[145] The reader is left to infer that Coolidge's course could not have treated the rich cultural themes so central to mid-20$^{th}$ century Western Civ.

Yet the account of Coolidge's method Allardyce relies on actually says something like the opposite of this.[146] Coolidge advocated fact-based lectures and quizzes in section, yes, but these were a foundation for challenging term papers based on independent library research. Coolidge required students to master a spare, fact-based book of key dates and events precisely because he rejected more ambitious textbooks in favor of independent reading from primary sources and scholarly works.[147]

In addition to his long and distinguished teaching career, Coolidge served as Director of Harvard's library and was largely responsible for building its world-class modern collection. Friends called the library Coolidge's "cathedral," and he was known for inspiring a love of libraries, books, and book collecting in students like Franklin D. Roosevelt. (Coolidge was Roosevelt's freshman advisor and gave him a B in History I.)

Coolidge looked at textbooks (like the ones used in many mid-20$^{th}$ century Western Civilization classes) as too elementary for students whom he believed ought to be learning techniques of advanced independent research. Far from being stunted by superficial facts, Coolidge's students used their firm factual foundation to explore the best available scholarly writing on European history. Coolidge's approach is clearly

---

144  Ibid., pp. 703-709.
145  Ibid., p. 701.
146  See Coolidge's remarks to the American Historical Association in 1898, "The New Haven Meeting of the American Historical Association," *American Historical Review*, Vol. 4, 1898-1899, pp. 413-414; Allardyce, "Rise and Fall," p. 701.
147  Here and in the material below I draw on Robert F. Byrnes, *Awakening American Education to the World: The Role of Achibald Carey Coolidge, 1866-1928*, (Notre Dame: Notre Dame Press, 1982), esp. pp. 37-39, 89-105, 135-147.

a modern variation on Harvard's 18th century technique of combining memorization of fact-based introductory surveys with recourse to the very best sources at the library. Contemporary scholars looking to portray traditional American education as outmoded and hidebound consistently miss or misread this technique.

Coolidge was also his era's greatest advocate for the then-unfashionable study of non-Western history. Yet that didn't prevent him from seeing the study of European history as the indispensable foundation for a liberal education and the necessary basis for understanding both America and the world. Coolidge's special interest was political and diplomatic history, yet he insisted that students could not understand these subjects without a broader understanding of issues like religion and ethnicity.

In short, Coolidge's History I was a Western Civilization course if ever there was one. Very arguably it was a more sophisticated version of Western Civ than many of the textbook-based courses of the mid-20th century.

When Coolidge began co-teaching History I in 1893, the course covered Europe from the fall of Rome to the French Revolution. After offering a successful special section for students lacking knowledge of ancient history, Coolidge was given sole responsibility for the course. Here we can see in motion the condensation of the heretofore dispersed Western Civilization curriculum into a single class, as familiarity with the ancients at both the high school and college level began to fade.

Allardyce knows full well that some scholars attribute the founding of the modern Western Civilization course to Coolidge and his students, yet dismisses this with the claim that History I was just a rudimentary point of departure for Columbia's definitive innovations. Allardyce's misreading here is even more obvious in light of *Awakening American Education to the* World, Robert Byrnes's study of Coolidge's influence, published in 1982, the very same year as Allardyce's essay.[148] While Allardyce has been endlessly quoted since 1982, students of curricular history have essentially ignored Byrnes's book on Coolidge.

Yet Byrnes's fuller portrayal of Coolidge's course reveals Allardyce's account as a caricature. Equally important, Byrnes traces the national effects of History I, reviewing the teaching of the

---

148  Ibid. See also the article where Byrnes first attributes the introduction of a Western Civilization course at Harvard to Coolidge: Robert F. Byrnes, "Archibald Cary Coolidge: A Founder of Russian Studies in the United States," *Slavic Review*, Vol: 37, No. 4, Dec. 1978, pp. 651-667.

more than fifty former Coolidge students who introduced Western Civ courses at colleges from Bowdoin to Berkeley.[149] Former Coolidge students began teaching their own versions of History I as early as 1905 (at Princeton and Berkeley), so a second generation of this model Western Civ course had spread well before the First World War.

Much is made of the fact that graduates of Columbia's history program produced the lion's share of Western Civ textbooks in the mid-20th century.[150] Given Coolidge's jaundiced view of textbooks, his intellectual progeny would not have followed that path. Yet a group of Coolidge's one-time students did indeed edit the Berkshire Studies in European History, which came into wide use just as Western Civ was sweeping the country in the 1920s and 1930s.[151] Rather than textbooks, these were extended studies of particular topics in Western Civ, written at a college level. This was the Coolidge way, inviting students to supplement lectures and brief textbook summaries with work of far greater depth. Rightly understood, therefore, Coolidge's History I was every bit as much a direct ancestor to the mid-20th century efflorescence of Western Civ as Columbia's Contemporary Civilization course. And it all began a quarter-century before World War I.

The Allardyce thesis as filtered through Levine has become the common wisdom of today's historians. Consider this account of the battle over Stanford's Western Civilization requirement from *A War for the Soul of America*, Andrew Hartman's 2015 history of our recent American culture wars:

> Of course the conservative reaction to Stanford's revised curriculum was exaggerated…. The idea that the Western Civilization course represented a longstanding tradition was patently false…. the Western Civilization course was a recent American invention. Prior to World War I Americans had sought to distinguish themselves from Europeans, a desire the nation's humanities curriculum tended to echo. But when American politicians committed the United States to war in Europe, American curriculum builders followed suit, hitching the nation's cultural fate to Europe. (Here Hartman cites Levine.)[152]

---

149   Byrnes, *Awakening*, pp. 135-147.
150   Daniel A. Segal, "'Western Civ' and the Staging of History in American Higher Education," *American Historical Review*, June 2000.
151   Ibid., p. 139; Robert C. Binkley, "Review of *Berkshire Studies in European History*," *The American Historical Review*, Volume 37, Issue 1, 1 October 1931, pp. 89-90.
152   Andrew Hartman, *A War for the Soul of America: A History of the Culture Wars*, (Chicago: The University of Chicago Press, 2015), p. 229.

We have seen that the claim of curricular disinterest in Europe prior to World War I cannot stand. More than that, there is reason to wonder whether this by now conventional summary of the Allardyce thesis accurately conveys even the substance of Allardyce's original argument.

## Dubious Goods

After dismissing Coolidge's History I of the 1890s as a mere "point of departure," Allardyce turns to the direct inspiration for Columbia's 1919 Contemporary Civilization course (which he takes to be the "mother" of modern Western Civ).[153] Allardyce finds that inspiration in the work of James Harvey Robinson, a professor at Columbia from 1895 to 1919.[154] Robinson reorganized Columbia's introductory undergraduate General History course as early as 1900. Then, in a graduate course he taught from 1900 to 1915, Robinson worked out a thematic approach to Western history focusing on the development of modern rationalism, science, and liberal values. This vision guided Robinson's influential 1902 high school and college European History textbook, the first edition of which sold an impressive 250,000 copies.[155] Allardyce identifies Robinson's work as the intellectual prototype of Columbia's 1919 Contemporary Civilizations course, and of the nation-wide interest in Western Civ that followed the First World War.

It could be argued, therefore, that Allardyce actually attributes the "invention" of Western Civilization to James Harvey Robinson around 1902, well over a decade before America entered World War I. Allardyce seems to be trying to finesse this problem when he says: "So, *before* the First World War, American educators were prepared intellectually for the coming of the Western Civ course. What prepared them emotionally was the war itself. During the Great Crusade, historical perceptions of a pioneer America, formed by the frontier experience, gave way to an alternative vision of the nation's connection with Europe."[156] [My emphasis]

We have established that Allardyce and Levine have vastly exaggerated the shifting American vision of Europe supposedly brought on by

---

153   Allardyce, "Rise and Fall," p. 703.
154   Ibid., pp. 704-709.
155   Segal, "'Western Civ' and the Staging," p. 780.
156   Allardyce, "Rise and Fall," p. 706.

the First World War. In the absence of that change, the pre-war roles of Robinson, Norton, Coolidge, and the miniature army of Coolidge's successors looks more significant. Even at Harvard, birthplace of the elective system, the gap between Henry Torrey's course featuring classics like Robertson and Guizot and Coolidge's History I was only about 20 years (1871-1892). In between, Harvard's Edward Channing taught a European history survey that was indeed largely focused on mastery of facts about political, military, and diplomatic affairs.[157] Even at Harvard, then, the broader "civilizational" approach went into eclipse for only a couple of decades, during which time a European history survey was offered nonetheless.

But can we at least say the Great War produced a significant upsurge of interest in Western Civilization classes? The single existing direct scholarly critique of Allardyce argues that even this is not quite so. In 2000, Pitzer College Anthropologist Daniel Segal published "'Western Civ' and the Staging of History in American Higher Education" in the same journal where Allardyce's original piece appeared.[158] Segal offers no challenge to Allardyce's claim that Western Civ was absent from America's college campuses prior to World War I. In fact, Segal pushes the effective date of the course's debut from 1919 to 1926, when a cascade of Western Civ textbooks published by Robinson's former students appeared. In doing so, however, Segal shows that the connection between World War I and Western Civ is far more tenuous than Allardyce claims.

Having examined the records of Columbia's famous War Issues Course, Segal reports that it covered only the war's immediate causes and traced those merely to the preceding decades. Segal concludes that Columbia's War Issues Course was not, in fact, "a sweeping survey of the West's civilizational lineage."[159] And having studied the syllabus of Columbia's 1919 Contemporary Civilization class, Segal finds that little of it was devoted to historical narrative. Even there, coverage only went back as far as the 18th century. As Segal puts it, "Allardyce's account of Western Civ's emergence at Columbia in the midst of and immediately after the war is a dubious piece of goods."[160]

Accounting for the popularity of the Allardyce thesis among historians, Segal hits the nail on the head when he explains that "the linkage

---
157 Byrnes, *Awakening American Education*, p. 37.
158 Segal, "'Western Civ' and the Staging," pp. 770-805.
159 Ibid., p. 781.
160 Ibid., p. 786.

of Western Civ to U.S. militarism seems a self-evident truth to those of us living in the shadow of the 1960s."[161] Segal's "us" is apt, since his critique of Allardyce merely serves as the opening for a still more radical effort to "unsettle" the traditional Western narrative. Segal argues for replacing the rubric of "civilization" with a relativist and globalizing treatment of world history. Rather than presenting the free market as an outcome of historical progress, for example, Segal wants textbooks to point to the exchange systems of non-Western peoples as intimations of a future without capitalism.[162] From Segal's perspective, while Allardyce might have been mistaken about the specific effects of World War I on the popularity of Western Civ, Allardyce's contention that the Western Civilization course is a latter-day invention still stands.

And Segal does substantiate a weaker form of Allardyce's claims about World War I.[163] The raft of Western Civ textbooks that emerged between the two World Wars did in fact stress the dangers of a resurgent barbarism in Europe, of which the savagery of the First World War was taken as a prime example. So over the long term, World War I may indeed have helped stimulate renewed interest in the survival of Western civilization. And that broader preoccupation with the fate of the West between the two world wars may have helped promote the idea of a required general education course in Western history. Yet it's evident that Norton's and Coolidge's highly influential teaching and Robinson's popular textbooks had begun to restore the older civilizational approach to history well before World War I.

Although Segal's work renders Allardyce's claims about the invention of Western Civ as a kind of propaganda tool to promote World War I untenable, scholars continue to make the point as if Segal had never written this article.[164] Even setting the war issue aside, the broader "invention" claim will never disappear so long as the pre-World War I history of Western Civ remains hidden and unacknowledged. Remarkably, Segal is one of the rare contemporary scholars who has actually read Herbert Baxter Adams's study of 19th century history courses.[165] Yet Segal appears not to recognize the work of Robertson

---

161  Ibid., p. 785.
162  Ibid., p. 799.
163  Ibid., pp. 786-788.
164  Hartman, *A War for the Soul of America*, p. 229; Rothman, "The Problem With Rep. Steve King's Take."
165  Segal, "Western Civ' and the Staging," p. 774.

and Guizot, whose widely-taught texts focusing on social and cultural themes are cousins to the mid-20th century Western Civ textbooks written by Robinson and his students.

So it would appear that Western civilization was not invented during World War I but has been around far longer, and has been taught for quite some time as well. Before we dive in and explore the implications of the lost pre-1917 story of Western civilization for our understanding of recent history and of who we as a society are now, let's take stock.

## Breathe Life

It's apparent that entirely too much significance has been attributed to the term "Western civilization," and to whether that phrase happens to stand as the formal title or topic of a single college course or textbook. The expression "Western civilization" was being used unselfconsciously by at least 1890. The growing use of this term in the ensuing years was a way of acknowledging the emergence of the United States as a player on the world stage. No longer would America be considered a youthful extension of a common "European civilization." As a mature power on its own continent, the United States would henceforth be considered a significant force within a broader cultural zone called the West.

Yet the difference between the United States conceived as part of a widely-dispersed "Western civilization" or as an adventurous extension of "European civilization" onto a new continent is not very large. And given that the term "European civilization" was long contrasted to the civilizations of "the East," the idea of a "Western" civilization was latent, so to speak, even before it came into common use. Broadly speaking, whether we call it "Western civilization," European civilization," or even, as often in the 18th and 19th centuries, merely "civilization" (under the assumption that European society was at the leading edge of general human progress), the basic cultural and historical referent for purposes of college teaching and otherwise was essentially the same.

The shift from "Christendom" to "Europe," on the other hand, was more consequential. Where the idea of Christendom dominates, the subject of history also differs in important respects. Although there is a significant overlap between Jonathan Edwards' recounting of history and what later came to be called Western Civilization, Edwards' narrative was largely built around God's redemptive actions, in contrast to the more secular histories that followed. This, however, does nothing to gainsay deeper civilizational continuities, such as those pointed out by Guizot (e.g. the connection between the early Christian affirmation of the equality of believers before God and the modern idea of political equality). So while it makes sense to distinguish the modern and more secular idea of civilizational history from an earlier and more religious mode of thinking, we ought not posit an irrevocable break in the continuity of Western civilization itself. Nor should we forget that relatively more secular treatments of civilizational history by Robertson (a clergyman) and Guizot remained compatible with religious faith, and even included a place for Providence.

The word "civilization" is an interesting and important cultural-historical marker, yet its significance should not be exaggerated. American college students have been studying European "civilization" ever since Adam Ferguson made the first use of that word in English. And Montesquieu's earlier "spirit of the laws" or "general spirit" of a given society amounted to much the same thing as "civilization," as did Jonathan Edwards' even earlier reference to the "civilized nations" of Christendom.

The over-valuation of terminological shifts betokens contemporary historians' loss of confidence in the reality of tradition, and consequently in the meaning and significance of history itself. The preference of contemporary historians for debunking and deconstruction has become at least as much of a blinding orthodoxy as earlier historians' bias toward continuity. If modern-day historians had devoted even a tenth of the effort to exploring continuities that they now put into exposing so-called invented traditions, the Allardyce thesis would have been overturned long ago.

America's college students have been reading the Great Books and studying the history of Western civilization since before the Revolution. Princeton in the 1760s and 70s and Harvard between about 1820 and 1840 may have pioneered more recognizably modern pedagogical approaches to the classics and to history, yet even in the era of heavy-handed discipline and mandatory memorization the richness of the classics came through.[166] We underestimate the usefulness of memorization, which when rightly done can turn a classic poem or great oration

---

166 Carl J. Richard, *The Founders and the Classics: Greece, Rome, and the American Enlightenment*, (Cambridge, Massachusetts: Harvard University Press, 1994), pp. 12-38.

into a cherished lifetime possession. And even in the 18th century, the most effective and inspiring teachers avoided the rod and breathed life into their subjects.[167]

## One-Sided Game

Many of the Founders ended their formal schooling having established lifelong friendships, so to speak, with their favorite classical authors.[168] John Adams took Cicero as both a personal counselor and the model for his career; while Jefferson's greatest pleasure in retirement was reading Tacitus and Homer.

All three of those authors were on the required or recommended reading list of the Stanford Western Culture course that was eliminated in 1988.[169] Those who favored Stanford's Western Culture requirement never claimed that the school's Great Books list designated a complete or fixed canon. Nonetheless, the overlap between America's traditional college curriculum and the Stanford list of 1988 is striking.

Candidates for college admission in the Founding era had to translate selections from Cicero, Virgil, Homer, and the Greek New Testament, all of which were on Stanford's 1980s list. Madison prepared for college by reading Thucydides and Plato, also on the Stanford list. Cicero, Virgil, Homer, and the New Testament were at the heart of the pre-Revolutionary college curriculum, with Demosthenes, Plato, Horace, and Livy formidable presences as well.[170] Of these latter readings, Plato took on greater importance in the 19th century and remained a major force in the Stanford Great Books curriculum of the 1980s.[171] Locke was the Enlightenment thinker who appeared most widely in the pre-Revolutionary curriculum, and he had a place on the Stanford Great Books list as well.

Greek tragedies rose to prominence in the American college curriculum after the 1820s, and were represented over a century-and-a-half later at Stanford.[172] Later writers on the Stanford list, such as Karl Marx

---

167   Ibid.
168   Ibid.
169   Mary Louise Pratt, "Humanities for the Future: Reflections on the Western Culture Debate at Stanford," in Darryl Gless and Barbara Herrnstein Smith ed., *The Politics of Liberal Education*, (Durham: Duke University Press, 1992), pp. 17-18.
170   Robson, *Educating Republicans*, pp. 81-82.
171   Winterer, *The Culture of Classicism*, pp. 65, 123.
172   Ibid., p. 92.

and John Stuart Mill, may not have been read at American colleges in the mid-19th century, but Guizot, whose understanding of social class and of liberty so profoundly influenced Marx and Mill, was. Johann Wolfgang von Goethe, on the Stanford list of the 1980s, was a major inspiration for the "philhellenic" movement that transformed the classical curriculum in the 1820s.[173] Charles Eliot Norton's assignment of Homer, Dante, and Shakespeare in the 1890s was echoed at Stanford nearly a century later, as Shakespeare had been assigned in Madison's oratory course nearly a century before. Writing off America's early curriculum with a simplistic caricature of 18th and 19th century pedagogy is a clever way of obscuring the profound break that occurred with the abandonment of common reading assignments in the Great Books.

Notwithstanding the early dominance of the classical curriculum, required assignments of the Great Books have long been paired with historical instruction on the course of European civilization from the ancients through the moderns. Cornelius Felton may have advanced the cause of ancient history in the early 19th century with his carefully chosen Greek excerpts from Herodotus and Thucydides, but the Founding generation was already steeped in ancient history and drew on it continually.

The great Enlightenment histories of modern Europe by Ferguson and Robertson first broke into the curriculum at pre-Revolutionary Princeton and Harvard, the two academic centers of patriot sentiment.[174] Robertson's presence in the curriculum broadened throughout much of the 19th century, spurred on by influential figures like Jefferson and Sparks. Montesquieu's "invention" of the modern idea of Western civilization, a vision broadly continuous with the 20th century college course, was assigned at pre-Revolutionary Princeton and was formally taken into the Harvard curriculum shortly after the Revolution. The Founding generation as a whole was intimately familiar with Montesquieu and far more influenced by Robertson than most have realized.

Charles Eliot Norton's early attempt in the 1890s to condense the entire development of Western Civilization into a single course may have brought the notion of civilizational continuity to the fore, yet that idea was hardly new. The Founders would have had neither the wisdom nor the courage to embark upon their great experiment in

---
173   Ibid., pp. 31, 82.
174   Robson, *Educating Republicans*.

self-government without the example of the ancients, a predecessor society they felt tied to in the most personal way. At the same time, under the influence of Enlightenment ideas, the Founders broke with the ancients in important respects, and knew they were doing so.[175]

That ambiguity never disappeared. From the philhellenes of the 1820s, through Norton in the 1890s, to Allan Bloom in the 1980s, the ancients have remained, simultaneously, indispensable precursors, imperfect predecessors whose limitations we have sought to transcend, and models against which we may measure our own limitations.

The idea of Western civilization has never posited a single continuous society from Moses and Socrates to the present, but rather a chain of influences that connect but also distinguish different social eras. Robertson and Guizot began their histories with the fall of Rome, the better to trace the influence of the ancient world on modern Europe. They assumed that their classically educated listeners would understand the earlier historical course of the moral, legal, municipal, and religious influences they traced from the moment of Rome's fall. Modern Western Civilization courses simply made this continuity between the ancients and moderns more explicit.

A persuasive critique of the idea of Western civilization would first have to venture a balanced assessment of the chain of influences, powerful continuities, and equally significant cultural discontinuities that extend from the ancient world to the modern West. Only on the basis of a vision of what Western civilization *is* can you rightly show what it is not. But of course proceeding along these lines would require conceding a certain reality to the concept of Western civilization, precisely what deconstructionist historians are aiming to avoid.

Yet without such a concession, deconstructionist techniques cannot help but lead to error and incoherence. The vision of a globalizing multicultural world rests on the idea of distinct cultures. If there is no such thing as a distinctive Western civilization, then the idea of a gradually increasing intermixture of cultures—the very premise of "globalization"—makes no sense. If the West is gradually being globalized, historians are obliged to generate an account of a culturally distinctive West against which the progress of globalization can be assessed.

---

[175] Paul A. Rahe, "Cicero and the Classical Republican Legacy in America," in Peter S. Onuf and Nicholas P. Cole ed., *Thomas Jefferson, the Classical World, and Early America*, (Charlottesville: University of Virginia Press, 2011), pp. 248-264.

Instead, the new globalist history has degenerated into a one-sided game whose implicit goal is to debunk the notion that Western culture exists at all. Every European borrowing of a new foodstuff, each trans-Atlantic disease transmission, or any artistic inspiration drawn from another continent is taken as proof of a culturally borderless world. Yet the significance of inter-cultural borrowing cannot truly be reckoned without a vision of what Western culture is to begin with. To what extent was early 20$^{th}$ century European art shaped by African ritual masks and sculpture, and to what extent were African representational techniques simply recruited to artistic projects animated by profoundly Western premises?

The new globalist history makes the same error in space that the notion of a Western civilization "invented" during World War I makes in time. Deconstructionist history assumes what it is trying to prove by focusing intently on cultural borrowing or on novel social conceptions, without assessing these innovations against what existed beforehand. By closing its eyes to continuity, deconstructionism can see only change.

## Inventor

Political philosophers are remembered in ways that historians are not. Mill and Tocqueville are re-read, and researched, and their influences are traced, while Robertson and Guizot have largely been forgotten. (Hume, that rare philosopher who was also a historian, is remembered far more for his philosophy than his history.) This leaves our picture of the development of American ideas incomplete.

While Robertson and Guizot were each progenitors of modern social science, they were not radically reductive or "historicist." Each conceded the role of choice in history and took the quest for the enjoyment of unalienable rights seriously. As such, their histories were compatible with American principles, as traditionally understood.

Yet to study Robertson and Guizot, as so many influential Americans did during the country's first century or so, was to absorb the American Creed through a distinctive lens. In reading these historians, Americans would have accepted both the principle of liberty and the justice of its extension to new lands. At the same time readers would have retained a healthy appreciation for the cultural prerequisites of liberal democracy, and would consequently have been wary of ambitious projects for constructing representative democracies where those preconditions were lacking. Equally, American readers of Robertson and Guizot would have been concerned to educate immigrants in the democratic history of America and the West, both out of regard for liberal principle and out of respect for the cultural importance of assimilation. In sum, Robertson and Guizot made it possible to combine adherence to American principles with a healthy appreciation for the role of culture in history. Historians analyzing the 19th century could benefit from exploring the largely neglected influence of Robertson and Guizot on American conceptions of democracy.

Lawrence Levine's flawed contrast between an "exceptionalist" pre-World War I America, preoccupied with itself and uninterested in Europe, and an internationalist mid-20th century America, is rooted in a fallacious caricature of American exceptionalism. Like many contemporary liberals, Levine treats American exceptionalism as a synonym for crude nationalism. On the contrary, American exceptionalism roots national pride in our extensive development of the principle and practice of liberty. This renders the long history of liberty's development from ancient Greece through modern Europe a matter of intrinsic interest for all Americans.

American exceptionalism is one of the complex pivot points in the course of Western civilization alluded to above. It can and must be understood as both continuity and change, describing an historical course broadly shared with Europe, in which the American context nonetheless pares back social barriers which had limited liberty's flourishing on the Continent. This was Lewis Henry Morgan's point.

Tocqueville's "invention" of American exceptionalism as an analytical concept (if not as a phenomenon) depended on his repeated juxtaposition of European and American ways in *Democracy in America*. From the beginning, then, American exceptionalism has only made sense in comparative perspective. To truly know America, you must know Europe as well. Tocqueville's hope that democratic localism and other American innovations could serve as models for France depended on the existence of a broadly similar social structure and cultural heritage in the two countries. Again, the very idea of America's difference from Europe rests on the assumption of an underlying similarity.

In a sense, Montesquieu "invented" American exceptionalism even before America existed by setting up a contrast between England and France in respect to liberty, and then implicitly holding out England as a model for the reform of France. Guizot laid out a similar comparison between England and France, and it was Guizot's suggestion that

America was working out the future of liberty still more fully that helped send Tocqueville on his quest. Americans are justly proud to be taken as a model by others, yet also and necessarily respectfully fascinated by the European experience out of which their own adventure in liberty has emerged.

America's persistent religiosity in the face of Europe's more rapid secularization has long been regarded as a classic case of American exceptionalism. Tocqueville was stunned by the contrast between France, where the Church and democracy were at war, and America, where Catholic priests were at the vanguard of democracy's defenders.[176] Obviously, our exceptional religiosity inclines Americans toward greater, not lesser, interest in the story of European Christianity. Robertson and Guizot address continuities between Europe's Christian past and its democratic present in ways that Americans, perhaps even more than Europeans, are primed to appreciate.

Charles Eliot Norton grounded "true patriotism" in America's ruling ideals of justice and liberty under law. This gave Norton both a perspective from which to criticize America's actions and a profound interest in the European roots of the principles he so cherished. Contemporary liberals seem to have lost their feel for the way in which classic American exceptionalism draws together national pride, a basis for self-criticism, and a respectful interest in our European past. This is because modern liberals have lost their feel for the way in which the transcendent principles of liberty and justice for all can be blended with gentler forms of national and civilizational pride. The liberal fear that immigrants from outside of Europe will be insulted by the teaching of Western Civilization reflects a loss of faith in the power of American principles to break down barriers of ethnicity and national origin. Unfortunately, this lack of confidence in our unifying principles only guarantees that the ethnic and civilizational divides those liberals so fear will proliferate.

In sum, the course requirement in Western Civilization was not the product of a propaganda ploy in support of the First World War. Nor was the subject matter new. On the contrary, required study of Western Civilization extends back to the colonial period, antedating the invention of the word "civilization." Confounding constructivist doctrine, the thing preceded the word. In sum, Allardyce's debunking account of the teaching of Western Civilization at American universities is itself an invention.

---

176  Tocqueville, *Democracy in America*, pp. 287-290.

# Part Two: How the West Was Lost

## Part Two: How the West Was Lost

This year marks the 32$^{nd}$ anniversary of Stanford University's fateful decision to eliminate its required course in Western Culture. That decision dealt a blow to the already fading fortunes of Western Civilization at American universities. It also supercharged the national debate over the postmodern academy, and served as a prototype for what later came to called "multiculturalism" and "political correctness."

The Allardyce thesis—the claim that the very idea of Western civilization was "invented" as a propaganda tool of World War I—was invoked in 1988 by Stanford professors who opposed the Western Culture requirement. Disseminated among the many scholars who followed the Stanford debate, the Allardyce thesis eventually helped to shape America's K-12 curriculum as well. Several scholars who played an important role in developing the College Board's revisionist and globalist AP European History curriculum of 2014 were influenced by Allardyce.[177]

The scholars who have drawn upon the Allardyce thesis to replace the history of Western civilization with the study of globalism and multiculturalism form a thread connecting the past several decades of American higher education. By following their work, the history of the modern university can be traced and the worldview of Allardyce's acolytes laid bare. Tracing the history of the Allardyce thesis will allow us to better understand what happened at Stanford in 1988, and to recognize the consequences of that event. Stanford's Western culture controversy was a kind of beginning—or at least a critically important inflection point—in our continuing culture war. Against all expectations, American politics today has become Stanford's culture war writ large.

## Curricular Anarchy

Let's begin with Allardyce himself. His article indicates he had a direct part in the collapse of the Western Civilization requirement at Stanford University in the late 1960s.[178] Through the 1950s, Western Civ was the most popular course at Stanford. By 1963-66, when young

---
177 David Randall, *The Disappearing Continent: A Critique of the Revised Advanced Placement European History Examination*, (National Association of Scholars, 2016), https://www.nas.org/articles/the_disappearing_continent
178 Allardyce, "Rise and Fall," pp. 720-725.

Allardyce served as a teaching staffer for Western Civ, the course had entered a steep decline. Stanford's senior faculty had lost faith in the very idea of general education—and implicitly perhaps, in Western civilization itself. Teaching was wholly turned over to low-level staffers like Allardyce, who "sabotaged" the common lectures and curriculum. Each discussion section was run independently, according to the interest of the staffer. As Allardyce puts it, "We thought, in teaching from personal perspectives, that we were deepening the course. Instead we were digging its grave."[179] The result was curricular anarchy. The commonality at the root of the course's appeal was gone. When students duly demanded an end to all course requirements at Stanford—Western Civ most of all—the faithless faculty surrendered.

Far from expressing regret for his role in the collapse of Stanford's most loved course, Allardyce's essay announces the obsolescence of Western Civ. The course had its moment, which was brief, historically conditioned, and decidedly untraditional. Now, says Allardyce, Western Civ is consigned to the unrecoverable past. That is, Allardyce claims he arrived at Stanford just in time to kill off a course fairly begging to be put out of its misery.

Yet in light of Allardyce's blind spots and misconstructions, it's hard not to wonder whether he might have been looking for a way to assuage some residual regret. Surely scholars of his generation will have valued Allardyce's reassurance that nothing of moment was at stake in the death of the old curriculum. And following Segal, reducing great traditions to the manipulative schemes of capitalists and warmongers "seemed a self-evident truth to those of us living in the shadow of the 1960s."[180] Hence Allardyce's appeal.

Although Stanford's once popular Western Civ requirement fell in the late 1960s, the faculty grew restive as students fled the humanities in the ensuing years. Between 1969 and 1979, the number of undergraduate majors in the humanities at Stanford dropped from 1,062 to 624, even as the undergraduate population remained stable.[181] Faculty concern and embarrassment grew when a British newspaper reporter who'd interviewed visiting Stanford students wrote that for most of them "the period between the Second Ice Age and the inauguration of John

---

179  Ibid., p. 723.
180  Segal, " 'Western Civ' and the Staging," p. 785.
181  Carolyn Lougee, "Women, History, and the Humanities: An Argument in Favor of the General Studies Curriculum," *Women's Studies Quarterly*, Vol. 9, No. 1, Spring 1981, p. 4.

F. Kennedy seems largely undifferentiated."[182] A new Western Culture requirement was approved in principle in 1976.[183] With various specialized tracks to choose from, the course would offer more flexibility than Stanford's earlier Western Civ class. Unity would be secured through a common list of great works designed to take up between one-half to two-thirds of the reading in each track. Stanford's required Western Culture course debuted in 1980.[184]

# Global Age

This curricular restoration was supported by Carolyn Lougee, a history professor who would serve as Stanford's Dean of Undergraduate Studies while the Western Culture controversy was heating up, from 1982-1987. Lougee had been one of the scholars invited by *The American Historical Review* to contribute a comment at the end of Allardyce's original 1982 article.[185] She offered an enthusiastic endorsement highlighting the pertinence of Allardyce's essay to curricular reform.

Lougee also expanded on Allardyce's thesis, arguing that the spread of Western Civ courses in the early part of the century could be attributed not only to the First World War, but to the need to assimilate the children of impoverished European immigrants then flooding into the United States. If Lougee was correct to say that Western Civ played a role in the assimilation process, that can hardly account for the so-called invention of the course, nor identify its true beginning. Arguably, reading Guizot in college helped assimilate earlier waves of immigrants. Yet only a fraction of Americans attended college in the 18th and 19th centuries, and these were generally the children of established families rather than unassimilated and impoverished immigrants. Western Civ may have always helped to assimilate immigrants, yet the topic had long been central to American education. However far removed from our immigrant ancestors, we Americans have always

---

182  Isaac D. Barchas, "Stanford After the Fall: An Insider's Perspective," *Academic Questions*, Volume 3, Issue 1, pp. 24-25.
183  William Chase, et al., "To Strengthen Undergraduate Education," *The Stanford Daily*, Volume 170, Issue 39, 18 November 1976, p. 5.
184  Barchas, "Stanford After the Fall," p. 25.
185  Carolyn C. Lougee, "The Rise and Fall of the Western Civilization Course: Comments," *The American Historical Review*, Volume 87, Issue 3, June 1982, pp. 726-729.

needed to be reminded of the history of liberty: its long trajectory; the difficulty of securing it; the danger of neglecting it; and the country's unique way of advancing it.

Although Lougee's twist on the Allardyce thesis failed to account for the so-called invention of Western Civ, it neatly supported her program of curricular reform. Lougee argued that a new, non-assimilationist curriculum was needed for the global age. Just as the "invention" of Western Civ had been appropriate for the European immigrants of the early 20th century, said Lougee, a multicultural program of general education should be crafted for the globalizing 1980s and 1990s.[186]

Lougee aimed not to eliminate general education requirements at Stanford, but to convert them into a vehicle for the new multiculturalism. (The word "multiculturalism" actually came into wide use in the United States only a few years after the Stanford Western Culture controversy—and in significant part because of it.)[187] Alarmed by the post-60s decline in humanities enrollments, Lougee counseled her leftist colleagues to back the revival of general education, while transforming its subject matter from within.[188] Although Lougee taught Stanford's revived Western Culture course, she saw the growing attacks on the requirement by black, female, Hispanic, and Asian students as an opportunity. In 1986, Dean Lougee delivered a report to the Stanford Faculty Senate that carefully invoked Allardyce's "invention" thesis, the emerging prevalence of non-European immigration, and globalization as rationales for sweeping aside the Western Culture requirement.[189] That prompted the appointment of a task force charged with designing a replacement. As a key figure on that task force, Lougee was featured in the *New York Times* article that kicked off the national controversy over Western Culture's elimination.

As the *Times* put it, "Carolyn C. Lougee...a member of the task force, wrote that 'the Western Civ course is not a timeless, eternal distillate of human wisdom'...Instead she contended that it arose from the need of the

---

186  Lougee, "Women, History, and the Humanities;" Lougee; "The Rise and Fall;" E. S., "Report of CUS on Area I Legislation Proposed by the Provostial Task Force," *Minerva*, Vol. 27, No. 2/3 (June 1989), pp. 223-225; Carolyn Lougee, "Statements Prepared for the Meeting of the Faculty Senate on 21 January 1988," *Minerva*, Vol. 27, No. 2/3 (June 1989), pp. 265-268.
187  David O. Sacks and Peter A. Thiel, *The Diversity Myth: "Multiculturalism" and the Politics of Intolerance at Stanford*, (Oakland: The Independent Institute, 1995), p. 1.
188  Lougee, "Women, History, and the Humanities."
189  E. S., "Report of CUS on Area I Legislation," pp. 224-225.

United States, flooded with immigrants after World War I, to forge 'a myth of a West that transcended every ethnicity and embraced them all.' "[190] The Allardyce thesis thus helped initiate Stanford's momentous change.

Lougee may have succeeded in replacing Stanford's required Western Culture course with a multiculturalist alternative, but her hopes of using this reform to resuscitate the humanities failed. Like Stanford's older Western Civ course, the revived Western Culture requirement of the early eighties was one of the most popular classes at the school. In contrast, the "Culture, Ideas, and Values" requirement that replaced it was a short-lived flop. Few of the junior faculty members who had advocated for the elimination of the Western Culture course were willing or able to design a compelling multiculturalist substitute. The new requirement lacked coherence. Students quickly lost interest and the course was put to bed.[191]

De facto curricular anarchy returned, and humanities enrollments have correspondingly dropped in the years since, at Stanford and across the country.[192] Western Civ courses were loved precisely because of their common reading assignments, and because they compelled students to grapple with works that forcefully posed life's fundamental questions. So why did Lougee's goal of crafting an equally well-loved multiculturalist requirement fail?

At root, it was because she and her young faculty colleagues doubted the very existence of culture itself, Western or otherwise. At any rate, they behaved as though they were in doubt. Yes, Allardyce's claim about the so-called invention of the Western Civ course turns out to be false, which undercuts the conclusions Lougee drew from his thesis. More deeply, however, the perspective from which Allardyce wrote—and the perspective which has come to dominate the academy in our era—leads its adherents to question the very existence of any human social reality beyond illusory constructs. Far from inspiring students, that view corrodes the soul.

---

190  Bernstein, "In Dispute on Bias."
191  Jenny Thai, "The IHUM Epic: Transformation of the Humanities at Stanford," *The Stanford Daily*, April 5, 2012, https://www.stanforddaily.com/2012/04/05/the-ihum-epic/
192  Mark Bauerlein, "Faculty in Denial about Own Role in Decline of Humanities," The James G. Martin Center for Academic Renewal, June 20, 2019, https://www.jamesgmartin.center/2018/06/faculty-in-denial-about-own-role-in-decline-of-humanities/

# Regimes of Truth

Some constructivists are more radical than others. Yet even those who in principle concede the existence of authentic as opposed to invented traditions do little to clarify the distinction.[193] In practice, constructivists focus on debunking, and do little to describe the workings of human social life.

In its most radical form, in the writings of the immensely influential French postmodernist Michel Foucault, constructivist thinking presumes that what is called *culture* or *society* is better understood as a system of "power/knowledge."[194] Such systems are neither true nor false but are instead "regimes of truth," exercises in domination that both create and are created by forms of knowledge.

Here "truth" is not a discovery about the world but a technique used by power/knowledge to suppress marginal groups. From Foucault's perspective, "knowledge" of culture or civilization can be neither accurate nor mistaken in the conventional sense. Rather, so-called cultural knowledge consists of "truths" manufactured in the service of dominant groups. There is no "real" Western civilization to be described or criticized. There is only talk about "civilization" that serves as a tool for suppressing the purportedly less civilized. From this perspective, history itself is the continuous invention of "knowledge" in the service of dominant groups. It's Allardyce all the way down. Apparent "knowledge" of Western civilization is nothing more than a tool by means of which elites send powerless young men to die in wars that advance the interests of the governing class.

Foucauldian thought swept the American Academy in the late 1970s and early 1980s—just as Allardyce was writing. And Foucault's paradigm has dominated ever since. It perfectly suits the multiculturalist movement's interest in questioning, debunking, and rejecting existing forms of knowledge.

Yet Foucault's thoroughgoing skepticism puts him in a bind.[195] His work is nothing if not political. Everything is bent toward resisting the current "regime of truth" on behalf of groups disadvantaged by the

---

193 Eric Hobsbawm and Terence Ranger, eds., *The Invention of Tradition*, (Cambridge: Cambridge University Press, 1983).
194 Michel Foucault, *Power/Knowledge: Selected Interviews and Other Writings 1972-1977*, ed. by Colin Gordon, (New York: Pantheon Books, 1980).
195 Jurgen Habermas, "Some Questions Concerning the Theory of Power: Foucault Again," in Michael Kelly ed., *Critique and Power: Recasting the Foucault/Habermas Debate*, (Cambridge: MIT Press, 1994), pp. 79-108.

dominant powers. Yet on what basis can Foucault justify his political commitments, much less specify what a new regime of truth ought to look like? The very notion of a regime of truth delegitimates any possible replacement. Foucault's political commitments clearly derive from the great tradition of Western political thought. Yet from his perspective, that tradition, if it has any reality at all, is accessible solely by means of our problematic regime of truth. It is unclear how Foucault escaped that regime in order to describe and critique it, or why his truth, rather than any other, should be believed.

Foucault's problems are our problems. Lougee ran into them when she tried to use Allardyce to sweep aside the old general education regime and build a new one. Lougee's task seemed simple enough. Educators around the First World War had allegedly invented a new body of knowledge suited to the challenges of that era: European immigration to America, and our wartime alliance with Britain and France. Lougee reasoned that we could likewise invent a non-assimilationist general education requirement tailored to the era of globalizing multiculturalism.

Yet early 20th century educators didn't see themselves as "inventing" Western Civilization. They rightly believed that they were describing a continuous tradition to which they and their students were deeply indebted. That conviction emboldened them to make Western Civ a requirement, and disposed their students to accept and even embrace that demand.

How can a self-consciously "invented" program of general education inspire a comparable sense of obligation? Won't it be stigmatized from the start as the new boss's corrupt regime of truth? (Isn't this already how multiculturalism's opponents think of it?) How can a new general education requirement inspire a sense of collective indebtedness and obligation when it begins by severing historical ties and eschewing the very idea that Americans share a common destiny? Like young Allardyce at Stanford in the 1960s, Lougee in the 1980s believed she was deepening Stanford's humanities core by jettisoning its unity. Instead she was digging its grave. A common story was abandoned, and Stanford students increasingly lost interest in the humanities as a result.

Foucault had the benefit of training at France's finest university, the Ecole Normale Supérieure, where he mastered the great works of the Western tradition. Foucault's political commitments and analytical framework flow directly from the great Western writers, Marx above all. Marx in turn drew his materialism from Epicurus, his historicism from Hegel, and much of his economics from Adam Smith, even as he repudiated their conclusions. Was Foucault hoodwinked by prior regimes of truth when he adopted and adapted earlier ideas, or is his own work evidence of the Western tradition's continuity?

Foucault could take his political commitments for granted, leaving them dangling from a worldview that rendered the very act of justification impossible. Yet the opportunity provided to Foucault by his Great Books education must be accounted for. To the extent that we dismiss Foucault's education as the mere machination of a "regime of truth," we descend into a paralyzing nihilism. Yet to the extent that Foucault's genuine mastery of the Western tradition enabled him to transform it, the educational theories of his acolytes are called into question. In that case the Western tradition would be real, accessible across the gulf of time and social change, and a wellspring of informed choice and action—for better or worse. If Foucault actually learned from the canon, then his intellectual achievement calls his nihilism into question. If Foucault was adopting the insights of his predecessors, and not just their self-serving ideologies, it would point to the existence of truths that endure across time.

## Sacred Books

Regardless of race, sex, or ethnicity, virtually any American student who can secure admission to Stanford is vastly more Western than not. To introduce these students collectively to the great books of the West is a way of making them powerful: of allowing them to know who they are, so that they may more effectively choose who to be. Enabling students to recognize and argue over what they hold in common across their differences; providing them with material that prepares them to think through the fundamental alternatives in life; permitting them to recognize their kinship with, and indebtedness to, predecessors who made them what they are; all of this is what turned the previous iterations of Stanford's Western Civilization requirement into the most popular class at the school.

It was precisely this popularity that provoked the attack on the course. Students who falsely believed that their race, sex, or ethnicity excluded them from the tradition felt derogated by the respect for the West engendered by the course. And junior faculty who had developed critiques of Western racism, sexism, and colonialism—as well as constructivist critiques of the very idea of tradition—faced suspicion from students drawn to the great books. So long as students read them in common, the great books won out over the debunking spirit the younger faculty was trying to instill in them. That is why the great books had to go.

The most perceptive argument offered by critics of Stanford's Western Culture course was that the list of great works (the Bible, Plato, Augustine, Dante, Machiavelli, Luther, Galileo, Voltaire, Marx, Freud, etc.) was treated as "sacred," that the books were in effect worshipped instead of being read critically.[196] Defenders of the list replied that there was nothing sacrosanct about this particular selection of readings, and that the books were hardly treated as gospel. After all, they criticize one another and can never be accepted as a uniform or orthodox whole.

The critics were onto something nonetheless. Stanford's required readings weren't worshipped as repositories of some narrow orthodoxy, yet they were rightly revered as a collection whose very differences drove readers toward the most fundamental and formative questions. The readings were sacred in the sense that a kind of sacredness attaches to the Constitution: as a font of America's values; as an essential text for active citizens and aspiring leaders; as a foundational blueprint that ought not be tampered with lightly; and as the framework that nurtures and channels our very differences. No society can exist without sacredness of this sort.

Yet the critics of Stanford's Western culture course very consciously set out to destroy the core list as a way of removing any taint of "sacrality" clinging to the class. That sacrality was both the source of the course's appeal and the enemy of the critics' debunking pedagogies.

Herbert Lindenberger, a professor of humanities at Stanford, highlighted the need to desacralize the course.[197] Like Lougee, Lindenberger envisioned a thriving new requirement in the multiculturalist and constructivist modes. Some tracks would focus on the West, while others would not. Greek classics might still be taught, but now with an eye to the ways in which subsequent eras had reinvented the image of

---

196  Herbert Lindenberger, *The History in Literature: On Value, Genre, Institutions*, (New York: Columbia University Press: 1990), pp. 148-162.
197  Ibid.

the ancients to suit their changing social needs.¹⁹⁸ Lindenberger's vision went unrealized, however. The reformed requirement lacked coherence and swiftly passed from the scene.

Lindenberger's account of Stanford's Western Culture controversy repeatedly invokes the Allardyce thesis, and his scholarly writings are in the same spirit. In his 1990 book, *The History in Literature*, Lindenberger repudiates efforts to "learn from history" or to recover the past "as it really was."¹⁹⁹ Instead, he says, we should think of history as "the process by which we 'construct' whatever pasts we deem serviceable."²⁰⁰ Although Lindenberger says he is finished with attempts to recapture "true" pictures of the past, his reductive account of the social needs that drove various eras to reinvent their traditions, necessarily makes claims about history "as it really was." To question reality is to stake a claim about what is real.

Alert to these paradoxes, Lindenberger concludes his book with an ironic dialogue in which he plays both interviewer and interviewee.²⁰¹ There he acknowledges, if only indirectly and seemingly in jest, the vulnerabilities of historical deconstructionism.

When Lindenberger's interlocutor persona asks his author persona if he's a relativist, the author replies, "I'm a relativist whenever institutions impose demands on me that I'm not prepared to meet."²⁰² That is to say, Lindenberger is a selective deconstructor, targeting only those powers and traditions he objects to. This is rather like the "strategic essentialism" propounded by postcolonial critic Gayatri Chakravorty Spivak: relativize and debunk the cherished ideals of the dominant culture while defending the reality and continuity of your own minority group.²⁰³ Deconstruction serves as a political tool, a strategy.

That is not always how it presents itself. Historical deconstruction cultivates and relies upon our modern prejudice in favor of cynicism. If it's ancient or admirable it must be a myth; if it challenges hallowed traditions, it must be true. The politics and cynicism of the debunkers protect them. Yet the transparently political motivation of historical

---

198  Herbert Lindenberger, "Statements Prepared for the Meeting of the Faculty Senate on 18 February 1988," *Minerva*, Vol. 27, No. 2/3 (June 1989), pp. 333-334.
199  Lindenberger, *History in Literature*, pp. 3, 5, 78, 83, 107.
200  Ibid., p. 19.
201  Ibid., pp. 211-220.
202  Ibid., p. 212.
203  Bill Ashcroft, Gareth Griffiths, and Helen Tiffin, *Key Concepts in Post-Colonial Studies*, (London: Routledge, 1998), pp. 77-80.

deconstruction means that any presumption on its behalf must be discarded. Lindenberger's mischievously ironic "interview" nicely deflects doubts about his relativism. Yet even he remains apprehensive.

Lindenberger's interviewer self asks his author self whether he worries that historicizing the classics may shortchange their accessibility and greatness. He asks if impugning the core rationale and legitimacy of literary study will drive away the legislators, donors, administrators, and students who keep the enterprise going. Then Lindenberger-the-interlocutor suggests that the interview has seriously undercut the core argument of Lindenberger-the-author's book. Whereupon Lindenberger-the-author gently acknowledges the force of these difficulties.

Thirty years ago, Lindenberger's interview with himself was cute, chiefly because the dangers seemed distant. Today, with humanities departments desperate for enrollment—and even altogether shuttered at a few schools—Lindenberger's playful dialogue is a touch more sobering. More important, Stanford's curriculum controversy and the university it created have become paradigms for American politics as a whole. The incoherence, fragmentation, cynicism, blind spots, and naïve hopes of the constructivist movement now operate on a wider scale.

## American Regime

Carolyn Lougee endorsed Allardyce's original article; expanded his thesis; used it to initiate and justify the replacement of Stanford's Western Civ requirement; and introduced Allardyce's idea into national debate. Herbert Lindenberger invoked Allardyce to argue for the replacement of Western Culture, and to puncture the sanctity of the Great Books. The third key figure to draw on Allardyce during the Stanford Western Culture debate was Mary Louise Pratt, Professor of Spanish, Portuguese, and Comparative Literature. Along with Anthropology Professor Renato Rosaldo and Professor of Classics and Comparative Literature Gregson Davis, Pratt taught the only truly new track of the ill-fated Culture, Ideas, and Values requirement. Before that, she had been a leader of the drive to replace the Western Culture course.[204]

---

[204] Mary Louise Pratt, "Humanities for the Future: Reflections on the Western Culture Debate at Stanford," in Darryl J. Gless and Barbara Herrnstein Smith ed., *The Politics of Liberal Education*, (Durham: Duke University Press, 1992), pp. 13-32.

Although Pratt invoked Allardyce to suggest the ordinariness of curricular change, she had more than an inkling of the immense civic task implied by the jettisoning of Western Civilization. Like others, she pointed to the rise of globalization and Third World immigration to explain the need to end the Western Culture requirement. Yet well before multiculturalism became a byword, Pratt understood that the change she and other young faculty members were pushing for implied a radical re-visioning of American civic life. While Stanford's administration desperately worked to deny the significance of its abandonment of the Western culture requirement, Pratt understood the significance of sweeping aside not only Western Civilization, but the very aspiration to a unified culture. Or, as she put it: "What can cultural citizenship and identity be in a radically plural society enmeshed in relentlessly globalizing relations? Can there be a transnational national culture? Can it be good?"[205] These are excellent questions.

Pratt and her co-teachers tried to answer those questions in "Europe and the Americas," their experimental course for Stanford's new Culture, Ideas, and Values requirement. When the *Wall Street Journal* got hold of the syllabus for "Europe and the Americas," it published a scathing condemnation that inveighed against replacement of the classics by fashionable leftist texts obsessed with race, class, and gender.[206]

In a letter to the *Journal*, Stanford's Assistant Dean of Undergraduate Studies, Charles Junkerman, shot back that while John Locke might have been an indispensable text for addressing the social justice question fifty years ago, globalization and the rise of Third World immigration means that work by a black Algerian psychoanalyst like Frantz Fanon is the best way to grapple with social justice at the present time.[207]

Allan Bloom, author of the best-selling 1987 critique of the postmodern academy, *The Closing of the American Mind*, dismissed Junkerman's claim as:

> the dogmatic and ignorant assertion that we have nothing to learn from old thinkers...[that] today's preferred answers are the only respectable answers. Locke's profound dissenting voice is silenced because 'we need' Mr. Fanon's racism and

---
205   Ibid., p. 16.
206   " 'The Stanford Mind:' Two *Wall Street Journal* Editorials," in Robert L. Stone, ed., *Essays on the Closing of the American Mind*, (Chicago: Chicago Review Press, 1989), pp. 362-365.
207   Charles Junkerman, "Stanford's Philosophy is an Open Book," in Robert L. Stone, ed., *Essays on the Closing of the American Mind*, (Chicago: Chicago Review Press, 1989), pp. 367-368.

incitement to terrorism, aping as it does, recent German and French writers. Inasmuch as Locke was and is the decisive philosophic source of the Declaration of Independence and the Constitution, we now know what Stanford thinks of the American regime.[208]

The Allardyce thesis is designed to disguise precisely these stakes in the battle over Western Civilization. Its message is that Western Civilization is a recent invention, and therefore sweeping it aside is of no great moment. America prospered before the idea of Western Civilization did, and will continue to thrive once that idea is gone, Allardyce implies.

He is mistaken. America and Western civilization were inextricably intertwined ideas and realities even before the birth of the United States. Casting Western civilization aside thus signifies a radical cultural break that places America's future in doubt. Although Pratt and her colleagues invoke Allardyce to disguise these stakes, she and Bloom both understand that we have entered a period of testing in which the survival of the American "regime" is up for grabs. Can there be a transnational national culture? Can it be good? What happens to our Constitutional fabric when John Locke is replaced by Frantz Fanon?

Pratt offers an answer of sorts to these questions in her 1996 essay, "Daring to Dream: Re-Visioning Culture and Citizenship."[209] The piece grew out of the "Europe and the America's" course, her experimental replacement for Stanford's Western Culture requirement. (This was the same course attacked eight years before by the *Wall Street Journal*.)[210] By the early 1990s, the word multiculturalism had come into general use in the U.S. One of the most interesting things about Pratt's article is that she explicitly refuses to define the term, then in its infancy.[211] Instead she says:

> Multiculturalism is not a goal or a stopping-off place, like affirmative action, it is a strategy, not an end in itself...

---

[208] Allan Bloom, "Educational Trendiness," in Robert L. Stone, ed., *Essays on the Closing of the American Mind*, (Chicago: Chicago Review Press, 1989), pp. 368-369.
[209] Mary Louise Pratt, "Daring to Dream: Re-Visioning Culture and Citizenship," in James F. Slevin and Art Young ed., *Critical Theory and the Teaching of Literature: Politics, Curriculum, Pedagogy*, (Urbana, Illinois: National Council of Teachers of English, 1996), pp. 3-20.
[210] Pratt's 1996 essay is based on an address delivered in 1991, three years after the dustup in the *Journal*.
[211] The word "multiculturalism" had long been in use in Canada, but was new to the United States in the early 1990s.

Multiculturalism doesn't have a referent. Precisely because it denotes a strategy, it is a highly contextualized term. What it 'means' in a given instance will depend entirely on the context—who the participants are, what is at stake, and what is possible."[212]

Pratt puts us in mind of Spivak's strategic essentialism and Lindenberger's strategic relativism. The implication is that multiculturalism is whatever works to the benefit of its advocates. Sometimes this might mean treating races, sexes, and ethnic groups alike. Sometimes it might mean the opposite. Sometimes multiculturalism dictates the deconstruction of traditions. Sometimes it supports the reverse. The test is what advances the interests of the advocates of multiculturalism. This is why the strictures of "political correctness" are so unpredictable and intimidating. And this is why the dark underside of multiculturalism is an unstable, inconsistent, and corrosive skepticism.

Here we have an answer to our question about America's future under the aegis of multiculturalism. In Pratt's framing, multiculturalism offers no vision that applies to all. As an interest-group strategy, it seems destined to accentuate divisions. "When people ask me what is in all of this for the white middle class," says Pratt, "I [say] emancipation from the sense of being at the mercy of consumption."[213] Pratt fleetingly hints here that socialism might reconcile otherwise divided sectors of society. Yet for the most part she seems unable or unwilling to justify or account for her multicultural "strategy," much less offer a convincing rationale for non-minority buy in. Pratt occasionally invokes "democracy." Yet like Foucault, the upshot of her work is to undercut and delegitimate the Western democratic tradition.

In its place, Pratt offers a vision in which the liberties nominally available to all Americans are unmasked as the property of a small but powerful *criollo* elite.[214] (*Criollo* is Spanish for a person born in Spanish America of European ancestry. Pratt is intentionally broadening the term by applying it all Americans of European descent.) That is, Pratt reframes the belief in universal individual rights

---

212 Ibid., pp. 10-11.
213 Ibid., p. 14.
214 Ibid., p. 16.

as a form of ethnic posturing by Euroamericans. Decades before this technique came into general use, Pratt reduced the promise of American democratic republicanism to a ruse of "white supremacy."[215]

Pratt suggests that even emerging terms like "diversity" and "difference" may be inadequate to account for certain social forms that could emerge under advanced conditions of globalization. She paints the picture of an America that might someday experience, "intractable [group] conflict and profound incomprehension," where "the idea of a social synthesis or community is not an option, nor is the idea of a single national form of expression or representation that will speak to/for all." In this future, "there is no shared discourse or concept of membership, no shared symbols, not even any stable meanings..."[216]

If intractable social divisions on this order strike us as frightening or abnormal, Pratt reminds us that they are common in Latin America. (We see them today in Europe as well.) Pratt appears to believe that immigration is destined to bring unprecedented social dissensus to the United States, yet seems almost to relish this, or at least she barely takes it amiss. Of course, the battle over this prospect has turned into one of our central political fault-lines.

Yet Pratt also denies that "balkanization" is an inevitable outcome of multiculturalism.[217] As proof she cites the overlapping character of identities. No-one belongs to a single group, so "intersections" of identity will inevitably create alliances.[218] Based on an address delivered in 1991, this essay clearly foreshadows the present. What Pratt does not predict are the new divisions and novel hierarchies spawned by "intersectionality." Today, the more victim classes you belong to, the higher you rank.

Nonetheless, however imperfectly, Pratt's nearly three-decade-old vision of a fully multiculturalist society anticipates many of today's conflicts. The future she "dared to dream" belies Allardyce's reassurance that nothing essential is at stake in the passing of Western civilization. If Pratt is right, then to exchange Western civilization for the multiculturalist alternative is to pull American tradition up by its roots. Nor is the multiculturalist option a true alternative. It is neither a systematic replacement for the Western and American tradition of liberty, nor can it be reconciled to that tradition through anything like

---

215   Ibid., pp. 7, 10.
216   Ibid., p. 18.
217   Ibid., p. 14.
218   Ibid., p. 8.

a stable synthesis. Instead, multiculturalism rests uneasily beside and against the American tradition. This is the source of our current conflicts.

## Bursting Supernova

The importance of the Allardyce thesis should not be exaggerated. It is but a single thread in a vast fabric of modern scholarship. To consider Allardyce is to sample just a bit of the postmodernist, deconstructionist, and neo-Marxist thinking that has dominated the American academy for decades. With the collapse of Western Civ requirements at colleges across the country, Allardyce's goal has been accomplished, and his idea has correspondingly faded from the scene.

Yet a couple of things mark the Allardyce thesis out as distinctive. Unlike most efforts at historical deconstruction, Allardyce palpably "did something." His essay helped unravel the core requirement of American general education, transforming the academic landscape in a way that scholars could not miss. For several months in 1988, the Stanford Western Culture controversy riveted the nation's attention. Then and afterwards, academics learned of the Allardyce thesis from the *New York Times*, and from accounts of the Stanford controversy published by Lindenberger, Pratt, and Lawrence Levine. The claim that the very idea of Western civilization was invented as a propaganda tool in support of World War I spread to scholars far and wide. In its day, the Allardyce thesis was a supernova bursting in the deconstructionist firmament.

There has also been a second act of sorts for Allardyce and his supporters. With the decline of Western Civ, World History courses have come to the fore. The subtext of these courses is the need to reframe traditional history to accommodate Third World immigration, along with the quest to cultivate "global citizenship." Allardyce jumped on this bandwagon, and so did his admirers.[219]

In 1994, the U.S. Senate voted 99 to 1 to condemn proposed National Standards in American and World History.[220] The standards sparked

---

219 Gilbert Allardyce, "Toward World History: American Historians and the Coming of the World History Course," *Journal of World History*, Vol. 1, No. 1, (Spring 1990), pp. 23-76.
220 Diane Ravitch, "The Controversy Over National History Standards," *Bulletin of the American Academy of Arts and Sciences*, Vol. 51, No. 3 (Jan.-Feb., 1998), pp. 14-28.

outrage, both because they were multiculturalist in spirit, and because they laid considerable stress on America's faults. Yet the push for World History and the new multiculturalism barreled on unimpeded.

That movement hit a crescendo of sorts around 2014 when the College Board, already focused on its new AP World History Exam, introduced revised curricula for its AP U.S. History, and AP European History programs. The new curricular frameworks "globalized" the content of these courses—that is, infused them with transnational themes. The AP U.S. History (APUSH) changes sparked a firestorm of criticism, while the AP European History (APEH) revisions set off protests as well.[221] After all, APEH, which has long since omitted the Ancient Greek, Roman, and medieval periods, is all that remains of Western Civ.

The new APEH curriculum globalizes Europe by emphasizing the depredations of colonial capitalism. Meanwhile, the new APEH omits, minimizes, or subtly undermines core themes of Western history: the development of Christianity; technological, intellectual, and scientific innovation; the history of liberty in Europe; and the development of parliamentary democracy in Britain. APEH soft-pedals the problems of Communism and operates on "soft Marxist" premises, offering debunking analyses of religion and liberal democracy as tools of powerful class interests.[222]

David Randall's thoroughgoing critique of APEH for the National Association of Scholars pointedly adds: "APEH never mentions that Americans should study Europe's past *because it is our history.*" [Emphasis in original] With Europe's central story and the most compelling reason for knowing it gone, what's left, says Randall, is flat language and sheer boredom.[223]

APEH could have been designed by the same scholars who created Culture, Ideas, and Values, the flop replacement for Stanford's Western Culture course. In fact it was. Carolyn Lougee, the historian and dean who used Allardyce as a rationale for replacing Stanford's Western

---

221 Stanley Kurtz, "How the College Board Politicized U.S. History," National Review Online, August 25, 2014, https://www.nationalreview.com/corner/how-college-board-politicized-us-history-stanley-kurtz/; Stanley Kurtz, "Why the College Board Demoted the Founders," National Review Online, September 9, 2014, https://www.nationalreview.com/corner/why-college-board-demoted-founders-stanley-kurtz/; Scholars Concerned About Advanced Placement History, "Letter Opposing the 2014 APUSH Framework," Posted at the website of the National Association of Scholars, June 2, 2015, https://www.nas.org/iwmages/documents/Historians_Statement.pdf; Randall, *Disappearing Continent*; Peter Wood, "The New AP History: A Preliminary Report," National Association of Scholars, July 1, 2014, https://www.nas.org/articles/the_new_ap_history_a_preliminary_report.
222 Randall, *Disappearing Continent.*
223 Ibid., pp. 31-32.

Culture requirement, was one of a handful of academics on the committee that designed the controversial APEH revisions. And the Allardyce thesis has had a marked effect on other College Board leading lights.

Social historian Peter Stearns has worked closely with the College Board for years. Stearns chaired the AP World History Exam Development Committee from 1999-2006 and co-authored a prominent AP World History textbook for the influential publisher Pearson.[224] In 2003, Stearns published *Western Civilization in World History*, a book that makes the case for infusing Western history with globalist themes.[225] This was a decade before the College Board moved decisively in that direction. Bonnie Smith, another one of the academics on the AP European History redesign committee, wrote the blurb for Stearns's book.

In *Western Civilization in World History*, Stearns draws heavily on the Allardyce thesis, as modified and developed by Lougee, Levine, and Segal, devoting an entire chapter to the issue.[226] Naturally, Stearns uses Allardyce to shake the reader's faith in the need to study Western civilization. Stearns plainly says he's a "convert" to the World History movement. In contrast to Pratt, however, he presents himself as a moderate who hopes to synthesize the story of Western civilization with world history, thereby doing justice to both.[227] The College Board's apparent efforts to carry out Stearns's program do not generate much optimism about the fruits of this moderation.

Bonnie Smith, the Rutgers University historian who helped design the new AP European History curriculum framework, co-authored a widely used textbook for APEH in the mid-1990s.[228] The senior author of that text was UCLA historian Lynn Hunt, a well-known historian of the French Revolution and a former president of the American Historical Association. In the preface to *The Challenge of the West*, Hunt and Smith recount the Allardyce thesis, putting students off their subject even before the main text of the book begins.[229] And as we've already seen, *Time magazine* had Hunt recount the Allardyce thesis in 2016 as a way of discouraging interest in Western civilization and supporting the rise of

---

224  Sharon Cohen, "AP World History Teacher's Guide," The College Board, 2006, p. 3, https://secure-media.collegeboard.org/apc/ap07_worldhist_teachersguide.pdf; Peter Stearns, Michael Adas, Stuart B. Schwartz, *World Civilizations: The Global Experience, Vol. 2*, (New York: Harper Collins College Publishers, 1996).
225  Peter Stearns, *Western Civilization in World History*, (New York: Routledge, 2003).
226  Ibid., pp. 9-18.
227  Ibid., pp. 1-6.
228  Lynn Hunt, Thomas R. Martin, Barbara H. Rosenwein, R. Po-chia Hsia, and Bonnie G. Smith, *The Challenge of the West: Peoples and Cultures from the Stone Age to the Global Age*, (Lexingon, Mass.: D.C. Heath, 1997), p. vii.
229  Ibid., p. vii.

World History in its place.²³⁰ The scholars who have crafted and influenced the College Board's controversial new curricula see the Allardyce thesis as a charter for a new, globalized version of history. Smith is now finishing up a book about "the global production of the West," while in 2014 Hunt published *Writing History in the Global Era*, a brief for globalism as the history paradigm of the future.²³¹

## Globalist Fallacies

Hunt's book on globalism begins with a survey of academic history as it stands today.²³² History as a discipline is in crisis, she says, intellectual as well as budgetary. Historical paradigms, from Marxism, to postmodernism, to identity politics have lost their vitality, says Hunt, leaving the discipline at sea. Although Foucault's influence is unmatched, Hunt notes, his rejection of truth, reality, and freedom now feels like a dead end. Today, Foucault's nihilism isn't so much contradicted as ignored, says Hunt. Yet nothing has taken its place. Historians, she concludes, have been "better at tearing down than rebuilding."²³³ None of this will surprise traditionalists, who've been making these points for decades. Yet here is a historian on the left and an acknowledged leader in the field nodding in agreement.

Hunt proposes globalist history as the solution. Thirty years out from Stanford, Hunt is feeling her way toward an answer to Pratt's questions: "Can there be a transnational national culture? Can it be good?" Yet globalist history turns out to be no solution at all.

Hunt presents globalization as a return to the grand historical narrative. Now history will have a purpose: "understanding our place in an increasingly interconnected world."²³⁴ Yet globalist history can't seem to get past square one. By Hunt's own account, no one can agree on when globalization began, or how to figure that out. Answers range from early man's departure from Africa, to the 1990s. The field also seems mired in

---

230  Rothman, "The Problem with Steve King's Take."
231  Lynn Hunt, Writing History in the Global Era, (New York: W. W. Norton & Company, 2014); Bonne Smith Faculty Biography Page at Rutgers History Department Faculty Directory, https://history.rutgers.edu/faculty-directory/professors/186-smith-bonnie
232  Hunt, *Writing History*, pp. 1-43.
233  Ibid., p. 39.
234  Ibid., p. 10.

a reductive materialism, which Hunt strives to overcome with limited success. The problem is that globalization as presented by Hunt is really only half a paradigm.

The nature, extent, and value of globalization can only be assessed with reference to the nations, cultures, and civilizations it connects. Since Hunt defines globalization as a process of ever-increasing interdependence, we need to know what societies that are more and less interdependent look like. We won't be able to decide when globalization began in earnest—much less what it means or whether it's good—until we can compare nations and cultures at various stages of the globalization process. But that would require the reconstruction of the very national and civilizational narratives deconstructionist historians have been trying to debunk for decades.

Globalization theory as currently constituted isn't a grand or purposeful narrative at all. It's merely deconstruction raised to the highest power. "The globe" sounds like an entity you can positively describe. Yet since there is no truly global society to speak of (John Lennon notwithstanding), shifting the frame of reference to the global level is simply a back-door way of undermining national narratives. Every imported foodstuff or borrowed custom is hailed as devastating proof that supposedly distinct nations and cultures are in fact thoroughly porous and interdependent—that nationhood itself is "imaginary."

This repeats the 19th century anthropological fallacy of "diffusionism." Diffusionist anthropologists traced the global spread of isolated cultural traits, as if this was the key to social wisdom. But diffusionists failed to address the reasons why a trait adopted by one culture was not adopted by another, or why traits would be adapted differently in different cultures. The issue is not the origin of isolated cultural traits, but how and why those traits are knit into the complex fabric of a given society. Figuring this out requires knowledge of culture. Globalization theory is the diffusionist fallacy on a grand scale. Even granting that renewed attention to global "flows" might be useful, nothing of significance can be concluded about the circulation of global goods and ideas until they're assessed with reference to the national cultures they're entering—and allegedly transforming. Given its political commitments, history as a discipline seems decidedly ill-equipped to make this intellectual move.

Writing in 2014, Hunt treated globalization as our inevitable future. Recent developments like Brexit and Trump have thrown this thesis into considerable doubt, and Hunt and her colleagues were as unprepared for them in 2016 as they were seemingly oblivious to the continuing significance of nation, culture, and civilization in 2014.

Following the thread of the Allardyce thesis sheds light on the nature of five decades worth of changes to the American academy. Contemporary dilemmas, however, have periodically seeped through that account, raising the question of what the Allardyce thesis, the aftermath of the Stanford Western culture controversy, and the lost history of Western civilization, have to say about the political-cultural struggles of our day. Let's take up these issues now.

# Part Three: Accusation and Its Discontents

## Part Three: Accusation and Its Discontents

Accusations of racism, sexism, homophobia, xenophobia, Islamophobia, and generalized bigotry have moved to the forefront of our cultural and political battles. Increasingly, the left half of the country calls the right half racist. The right half objects and takes the accusation itself as proof of extremism, bad faith, or bigotry in reverse. What has brought us to this point?

From a multiculturalist perspective, America is divided between minorities who may or may not want to be part of a given American definition of "we," and a majority culture that hates the "multicultural" "outsiders." In this view, the very act of naming and defining a common American culture is racist, insofar as it tramples on "multis" who resist assimilation and demand identities of their own. Lauding an allegedly common American culture as "great" compounds the offense, especially in light of slavery and other abuses of the past.

At first glance, this multiculturalist critique of America seems anything but relativist. The point, after all, is that Western civilization and its American offshoot have oppressed other cultures, preventing them from attaining the self-awareness and maneuvering room they require to flourish in all their distinctiveness. Beneath this surface of moral outrage, however, lies a pervasive skepticism about the reality of knowledge and culture—a skepticism that calls forth, paradoxically, an ever-deepening sense of moral superiority and certainty.

A curious blend of skepticism and moralism runs throughout this report. Gilbert Allardyce's deconstructive denial of the West's self-conscious civilizational continuity is simultaneously a critique of Western imperialist war propaganda. So, too, Michel Foucault conceives of "knowledge" not as an accumulation of insight into social reality, but as a "regime of truth" whose manufacture solidifies oppressive power. Foucault refuses to take "truth" seriously, yet implicitly presents his critique of it as not only true but as a morally compelling charter for resistance. Similarly, scholars who draw on deconstructionists like Foucault and Allardyce to ground and justify their turn toward globalist multicultural education engage in "strategic" essentialism, provisionally accepting the reality and continuity of non-Western cultures, even as the existence of the West—and indeed of culture itself—is denied. Yet the West, too, is periodically regarded as real, if only for purposes of condemning its depredations. The upshot appears to be that the West is evil; and besides, it doesn't exist.

Developing a fuller picture of the original battle over Stanford's Western Civ requirement is the way to understand the impact of this postmodern incoherence on the United States today. The conflict over the Stanford curriculum is where the changes born in the 1960s came to maturity, launching the culture war that divides America ever-more deeply each day.

## Hey Hey

Stanford's Western Civ requirement was abolished, along with all other course requirements, in the late 1960s. The required course was restored in modified form under the title Western Culture in 1980. Opposition to a revived Western Civ was present from the start, seemingly based on a desire to study non-Western societies. Many younger faculty members, particularly women and minorities, refused to teach the restored Western Culture requirement at all.[235]

Student opposition gained momentum during political organizing activity for Jesse Jackson's 1984 Rainbow Coalition run for the presidency. Stanford's rainbow alliance against the Western Culture requirement included the Black Students' Union, MEChA (Chicano students), the Stanford American Indian Organization, the Asian American Student Association, and Students United for Democracy in Education (largely, progressive white students).[236] This was a potentially substantial coalition, since close to forty percent of Stanford's undergraduate student body consisted of minority students.[237] Nonetheless, Western Culture remained Stanford's most popular course, a favorite of around 80 percent of the student body, many minority students included.[238]

Stanford's minority demographics were unusual in the 1980s. Nathan Huggins, Chairman of Harvard's African-American Studies department, said during the Stanford controversy, "I don't see black students at Harvard getting excited about this sort of thing."[239] Huggins pointed

---

235 Pratt, "Humanities for the Future," p. 22.
236 Ibid.
237 Lindenberger, "The History in Literature," p. 158.
238 Barchas, "Stanford After the Fall," p. 25.
239 Bernstein, "In Dispute on Bias."

to the large percentage of non-white students at Stanford as the reason for the discrepancy—although, again, by no means all of Stanford's minority students objected to the course.

Jesse Jackson came to Stanford on Martin Luther King Day in 1987 to address a rally of about 500 students and faculty on the university's central plaza protesting on behalf of their "rainbow agenda." In addition to abolition of the Western culture requirement, that agenda included calls for more minority student and faculty set-asides. As the crowd left the Plaza marching to present their demands to the faculty senate, they broke into a chant: "Hey hey, ho ho, Western Culture's got to go!"[240]

Although Jackson supported the students' proposed curriculum change, he preferred to frame it as an add-on. "There's more culture than Western culture," he told the rally, suggesting that their chant was too negative.[241] Actually, that chant was more direct and accurate than Rev. Jackson could afford to be. His presence at Stanford was preparation for his coming 1988 presidential run. That chant would not prove helpful with voters already skeptical of Jackson's politics.

Jackson had laid out his Rainbow Coalition idea three years before in a powerful speech before the Democratic National Convention of 1984:

> "My constituency is the desperate, the damned, the disinherited, the disrespected, and the despised…Our flag is red, white and blue, but our nation is a rainbow—red, yellow, brown, black and white—and we are all precious in God's sight. America is not like a blanket—one piece of unbroken cloth, the same color, the same texture, the same size. America is more like a quilt: many patches, many pieces, many colors, many sizes, all woven and held together by a common thread."[242]

Jackson went on to list various groups composing the Rainbow Coalition, each of them carrying moral claims on American compassion and generosity, grounded in their histories of oppression by racism, sexism, militarism, land dispossession, and so forth. While

---

240 Ibid.; Sacks and Thiel, *The Diversity Myth*, pp. 1-2.
241 Elaine Riggs, "Jackson calls for new Western Culture class," *The Stanford Daily*, Volume 190, Issue 59, January 16, 1987, https://stanforddailyarchive.com/cgi-bin/stanford?a=d&d=stanford19870116-01.2.3
242 Jesse Jackson, "1984 Democratic National Convention Address," American Rhetoric, https://www.americanrhetoric.com/speeches/jessejackson1984dnc.htm

Jackson agreed that we live in a "great nation," he added, "the rainbow is mandating a new definition of greatness:" how we treat the least among us.[243]

Although the word "culture" barely came up in Jackson's 1984 address, his speech before the Democratic National Convention of 1988 (likely influenced by the Stanford controversy) did feature a mention of the need for "different cultures" and "different civilizations" to meet and find common ground.[244]

Jackson's presidential runs were aimed more at gaining leverage for his constituencies within the party than for any likelihood of capturing the nomination. Some on the left saw Jackson's runs laying the groundwork for victorious multicultural coalitions of the future. Other progressives fretted that the Rainbow Coalition was "identity politics on steroids," and therefore liable to distract from the party's economic goals. Centrist Democrats viewed Jackson as the embodiment of all that was wrong with the party.[245] Convinced that identity politics and sixties-inflected leftism were alienating culturally traditional Reagan Democrats, Bill Clinton pulled the party toward the center in his successful presidential run four years later.

In retrospect, we can see Jackson's Rainbow Coalition as the forerunner of "the rising American electorate," the coalition of racial and ethnic minorities, women, and progressive whites that is believed to have won Barack Obama the presidency in 2008 and 2012.[246] Many of today's Democrats look to demographic change along these lines to restore the party to power and to keep it there for the indefinite future. It's important to recall, however, that not all Obama voters favored a strong form of multiculturalism. Indeed, some voices on the left continue to critique multiculturalism, and to call for a more economically focused approach instead.[247] Nonetheless, identity politics remains a powerful force, with California as its political-cultural center. Looking back, the unusual student demographics of Stanford in 1988 appears to be the beginning of the "rising American electorate,"

---

243 Ibid.
244 Jesse Jackson, "1988 Democratic National Convention Address," American Rhetoric, https://americanrhetoric.com/speeches/jessejackson1988dnc.htm
245 Robert Greene II, "Towards an Intellectual History of the Rainbow Coalition," Society for U.S. Intellectual History, October 19, 2014, https://s-usih.org/2014/10/towards-an-intellectual-history-of-the-rainbow-coalition/
246 Jesse Jackson Sr., "The Rising American Electorate is a Rainbow," *Souls: A Critical Journal of Black Politics, Culture, and Society*, Volume 14, 2012, Issues 1-2, pp. 67-72, https://www.tandfonline.com/doi/abs/10.1080/10999949.2012.723248?journalCode=usou20
247 Mark Lilla, *The Once and Future Liberal: After Identity Politics*, (New York: Harper Collins, 2017).

now imbued with an advanced version of the multiculturalism introduced at Stanford thirty years ago. That's one reason why the dynamics of Stanford's Western Culture battle are so closely intertwined with the controversies of our day, and require a closer look.

## Modern McCarthyism

Today it is taken for granted that charges of racism can and will be leveled not only at an arch-segregationist or a believer in genetic inferiority by race, but against almost any disfavored policy prescription or analysis. This was not always the case. The Stanford Western culture controversy served to normalize what we might call the "expanded" charge of racism—a charge designed not to condemn classic bigotry, but to discredit policy positions instead.

There had been a precursor in 1965, when the Johnson administration released a report by the future senator and then Assistant Secretary of Labor Daniel Patrick Moynihan. The Moynihan Report argued that black family life was caught up in a "tangle of pathology"—a self-perpetuating cycle of out-of-wedlock births, fatherless households, poverty, and crime—and that this cultural reality must be addressed by any proposed remedy for poverty. Moynihan was a liberal who advocated concerted government action to overcome black poverty, and he had taken the phrase "tangle of pathology" from noted black psychologist Kenneth Clark. Although he advocated liberal policies and had authored President Johnson's most lauded speech on race, Moynihan's report was condemned as a form of "genteel racism." He and his family were shunned in polite circles because of it for years. Although the mainstream press and Moynihan's defenders—many of them black—were scandalized by the charges of racism, likening them to a modern form of McCarthyism, the aggressive labeling worked. President Johnson distanced himself from the Moynihan Report and Moynihan's defenders fell away.[248] This incident was an early case of what would come to be called "political correctness," a quarter-century later. At the time, however, the Moynihan controversy—with its shockingly expanded charge of racism—remained something of an outlier.

---

240  James T. Patterson, *Freedom is Not Enough: The Moynihan Report and America's Struggle over Black Family Life from LBJ to Obama*, (New York: Basic Books, 2010).

Stanford's Western culture battle went the Moynihan flap one better. Moynihan had discovered that, intentions aside, pointing to problems in other people's cultures (or subcultures) is impermissible. Now the corollary was drawn: it is forbidden even to laud one's own culture, lest that imply derogation of others. Postcolonial theorists had been making a similar point for a decade before the Stanford dustup: however respectfully deployed, the culture concept creates an "us-versus-them" dichotomy that unavoidably denigrates "them." Yet this remained an obscure academic theory prior to Stanford's Western culture dispute. Today's multiculturalists likewise treat praise for traditional American virtues, or middle-class morality, as code for invidious racial, cultural, and class distinctions.[249] At a blow, this reasoning short-circuits America's ability to recognize, affirm, and transmit its core values. Culture itself becomes impossible. The very idea of a commonly held tradition is stigmatized as "racist." This logic first played out widely, publicly, and ruthlessly at Stanford in 1987-88.

Western civilization was attacked straightforwardly at Stanford in the late 1980s as racist, sexist, and imperialist. Yet the more damning complaint was something closer to the opposite of that. The real problem was that the great-books component of the Western Culture course was an immense success. Struggling through the great thinkers of the Western tradition was both a rite-of-passage for students and a way of grappling with the ultimate meaning of education, society, and life itself. That is why the course was so popular, and why the readings from Plato, Aristotle, the Bible, Marx, Freud, Voltaire, Darwin, etc. carried an air of the sacred about them.

For those students who believed their heritage excluded them from the West (although they were almost certainly far more Western than not), the absence of minorities and women from the reading list was a slap in the face. If you've decided from the start that you're non-Western, however, even adding minorities and women to the reading list won't solve the problem. So long as the great books are taken to be great; so long as they are read, not as cultural artifacts but as explorations of the fundamental alternatives in life; and so long as they are held up as the finest achievements of the West, the very appeal of the course becomes an implicit put-down of anyone who identifies as non-Western.

---

249  Jon Haidt, "In Defense of Amy Wax's Defense of Bourgeois Values," Heterodox Academy, September 2, 2017, https://heterodoxacademy.org/in-defense-of-amy-waxs-defense-of-bourgeois-values/; Peter Wood, "In Defense of Amy Wax," National Association of Scholars, August 8, 2019, https://www.nas.org/blogs/dicta/in-defense-of-amy-wax

Accusations of racism, imperialism, etc., thus became the battle cry of the course's opponents. The Moynihan precedent notwithstanding, this use of the racism charge to resolve an intellectual disagreement was novel and deeply shocking at the time. *The New York Times* reported that Amanda Kemp, former president of Stanford's Black Student Union, had charged in the student newspaper that the subliminal message of the great books curriculum was actually "nigger go home."[250] Nor was this an exception. It was also said at the time, for example, that the Western Culture course "is not just racist education; it is the education of racists."[251]

## A Simple Calculation

Sweeping accusations of racism of this sort had been bandied about for some time in the academy, where theorists of "systemic" or "institutional" racism had long since gained a foothold. Yet the Stanford Western Culture controversy was the first time so expansive a use of the racism charge had entered public debate at the national level, and on a topic—the great books—that for many bore no necessary or intrinsic connection to race. So Amanda Kemp's then-shocking claim that supporters of the Western Culture course were effectively saying, "N*****s go home," is worth a closer look.

Kemp's charge came in a reply to *Stanford Daily* columns by undergraduate supporters of the Western Culture requirement.[252] Those pieces expressed outrage over the proposed abolition of the requirement, chiefly because the proposed replacement would eviscerate the beloved great books component of the course. Yet these student op-eds bent over backwards to emphasize the importance of studying non-Western cultures and/or adding more readings authored by women and minorities to the existing course.[253] To claim these students were racists defied the common understanding of the word.

---

250  Bernstein, "In Dispute on Bias."
251  Barchas, "Stanford After the Fall," p. 25.
252  Amanda Kemp, "Blacks feel unwanted," *The Stanford Daily*, Volume 191, Issue 47, April 28, 1987, https://stanforddailyarchive.com/cgi-bin/stanford?a=d&d=stanford19870428-01.2.17&srpos=3&e=-------en-20--1--txt-txIN-blacks+feel+unwanted------
253  Editorial, ""Proposal is absurd," *The Stanford Daily*, Volume 191, Issue 41, April 20, 1987, https://stanforddailyarchive.com/cgi-bin/stanford?a=d&d=stanford19870420-01.2.18&e=01-03-1987-01-05-1987--en-20--1--txt-txIN-Western+Culture------# ; Scott Lyon, "Recommendations silly," *The Stanford Daily*, Volume 191, Issue 41, April 20, 1987, https://stanforddailyarchive.com/cgi-bin/stanford?a=d&d=stanford19870420-01.2.18&e=01-03-1987-01-05-1987--en-20--1--txt-txIN-Western+Culture------# ; David Risser, "Western

In leveling her accusation, Kemp acknowledged that her opponents may not have been consciously racist. Yet, she added, "they are responsible for their editorial's impact and implicit conclusions" nonetheless. Here was arguably the first introduction of the idea of unconscious or implicit racism into a high-profile national debate.

Kemp's core argument was that the Western Culture course made blacks feel unwanted. The upshot was that if the great books make minorities feel bad, they must be racist. We recognize this today as a widely-used argument in support of overly broad bans on campus "hate speech." Speech that makes students uncomfortable must supposedly be barred as hateful. Indeed, just after its Western culture debate, Stanford instituted one of the very first campus speech codes in the country (later found unconstitutional).[254] Much that is familiar today began 30 years ago at Stanford.

Yet a charge of racism used in the midst of a curriculum debate among students seemingly not so far apart on substance was deeply shocking at the time. And as with Moynihan, the charges worked. Once the accusations of racism went flying, the 80 percent of students who thought well of the Western Culture requirement faced a simple calculation. Keep silent and stay safe, or speak out and risk being publicly smeared as racist. Most kept silent.[255]

The expanded racism charge quickly became the lightning rod of the Stanford debate. Meanwhile, the *New York Times* article had made the "Western culture's got to go" chant nationally notorious. The issue, the chant, and the wild charges of racism soon drew President Reagan's Education Secretary William Bennett into the fray. Bennett spoke privately with proponents of the Western Culture course about the racism charges, and began to argue publicly that what ought to have been a reasoned debate was being settled through intimidation instead.[256] In part, Bennett was referring to the 1987 occupation of the office of Stanford's president by the Rainbow Coalition. Yet his larger concern was with the promiscuous charges of racism, which he and many at Stanford, and beyond, viewed as entirely out of keeping with thoughtful academic debate. Shocked by the accusations of racism against Moynihan, his supporters had called the tactic "McCarthyite."

---

Culture Tracks Suffice," *The Stanford Daily*, Volume 191, Issue 40, April 17, 1987.
254  Associated Press, "Court Overturns Stanford University Code Barring Bigoted Speech," *The New York Times*, March 1, 1995, https://www.nytimes.com/1995/03/01/us/court-overturns-stanford-university-code-barring-bigoted-speech.html
255  Barchas, "Stanford After the Fall," pp. 29-30.
256  Ibid.; "Bennett Charges 'Intimidation' in CIV Decision," *Minerva*, Vol. 27, No. 2/3, June 1989, pp. 391-411.

Proponents of Stanford's Western Culture course likewise rejected the racism charge as a "McCarthyite smear tactic" deeply at odds with university life. Regardless, it can fairly be said that generating charges of systemic, unconscious, and implicit racism (and associated other isms and phobias) is today a central preoccupation of America's universities, and increasingly a cultural dividing line in society at large.

## Never Fully At Home

To all appearances, the charges of racism at Stanford were meant to bring about a new course requirement focused on a wider variety of cultures. Yet there are signs that something very different was going on instead, signs that suggest there was no great interest on the part of the Rainbow Alliance or its faculty allies in the study of non-Western cultures. The charges of racism, in other words, were not a means to an end, but ends in themselves.

Consider an ideal-typical postmodern biographical profile—the story of Edward Said, founder of postcolonial theory and an important successor to Michel Foucault. (For more on Foucault, see Part Two of this report.) Said's 1978 book, *Orientalism*, has exercised more influence on the American academy than any single work of the past four decades.[257] The book is a root-and-branch attack on the culture concept that disallows almost any systemic representation of cultural "Others" as implicitly racist and imperialist. When generalized to a worldview, as *Orientalism* has been, truth-claims by Westerners regarding non-Western cultures are essentially ignored in substance while being parsed instead for evidence of implicit racism and the desire to dominate. This is essentially what Allardyce did with the idea of Western civilization. Mere talk of different cultures—and certainly, of "civilizations"—is in itself evidence of guilty "Othering." From this Foucauldian perspective, nothing particularly knowable exists beyond racism, sexism, neo-colonialism, "Orientalism," and other forms of oppressive thinking in service of "power." All is reduced to these multifarious sins, and the only salvation is to join Said in their unmasking. More insight into Said's perspective can be gleaned from his life-story.

Said had no real cultural home. Raised as a Christian by parents who were part American and part Arab; educated at an elite British colonial

---

257 Edward Said, *Orientalism*, (New York: Pantheon Books, 1978).

boarding school that forbade the use of Arabic; and sent alone to the United States to complete his education before he'd reached adulthood, Said became a loner, at home neither in America nor in the Middle East. By the time he became an academic, Said was so Americanized that he avoided the company of other Middle Eastern immigrants. Yet he never felt fully at home in the United States.[258]

It was the sixties that transformed Said. Taking up the mantle of Palestinian nationalism and protesting America's alleged imperialism in the Middle East bestowed on him a sense of Palestinian identity that he had never previously felt. Nevertheless, culturally, Said remained essentially American.

Said's invention of post-colonial theory provided a solution, of sorts, to his personal dilemma. Constant excoriation in writing of the neo-imperialist West acted as a nonstop sixties demonstration, so to speak. Politics allowed Said to continue to feel Middle Eastern, despite his sense of alienation from Arab culture. *Orientalism* is not an attempt to describe or explore Middle Eastern culture. On the contrary, it suggests that such a quest is both impossible and bigoted. *Orientalism* is, rather, a non-stop, almost monomaniacal search for racism/Orientalism/neo-imperialism hiding in so-called knowledge of the "Other." Attention to culture would, if anything, only embarrass Said, by reminding him how little Middle Eastern and how thoroughly American he was. For Said, identity is maintained through oppression narratives, not through the exploration of culture. The accusation of racism itself lends purpose, power, and character to the accuser, in a way that participation in some distinctive culture does not.

Like Edward Said, most minority students at elite universities are already culturally American, although of course they often share an ethnic heritage as well. For these students, deep study of African, Mexican, or various Asian cultures may be of some interest, yet it is by no means necessarily the key to identity. To a degree, such studies might even serve to remind minority students of how very American they actually are.

Narratives of oppression, however, reinforce a sense of identity and difference. Although Jesse Jackson touched on "culture" in 1988, his more powerful and memorable 1984 convention address was focused

---

258 Moustafa Bayoumi, Andrew Rubin, *The Edward Said Reader*, (New York: Vintage, 2000), pp. xi-xxxiv; Stanley Kurtz, "Edward Said, Imperialist," *The Washington Examiner* (originally published in *The Weekly Standard*), October 8, 2001, https://www.washingtonexaminer.com/weekly-standard/edward-said-imperialist; Edward Said, *Out of Place: A Memoir*, (New York: Alfred A. Knopf, 1999).

on the moral authority conferred upon minority groups by virtue of the collective historical suffering they've endured. Narratives of oppression, not explorations of culture, are the real keys to American minority identities. Charging non-minorities with complicity in that historical oppression is the new key to power. In a sense, it is the basis of a new kind of American culture.

Comfortably middle-class non-minorities can participate as well by empathizing and identifying with the causes of struggling minority-groups, but also by reimagining themselves as an oppressed class—the generation destined to bear the brunt of the chaos wrought by climate change, for example.[259]

Accusations of racism, in the new and expanded sense (subtle, almost invisible undertones of intellectual debate detectable only by the victim) have the effect of creating a new social hierarchy. The accused find it difficult to understand or predict which words or arguments may set off a charge. Almost anything is potential fodder for a racism claim. Accusations can be leveled for acknowledging differences, or for failing to acknowledge them. It is the minority player—his subjective feelings, and the historically-grounded moral claims of his group—that govern the new game. Arguments can be "won" by silencing opponents with subjective charges of racism too dangerous to dispute. Resistance only risks escalation of the charges and the loss of potential allies. Each incident of alleged "subtle" racism adds to the narrative of oppression, increasing the moral authority of the persecuted group while reinforcing its sense of collective identity.

America's minority identities, lacking roots in "thick" cultural differences—and otherwise dissipated by expansive opportunity and economic integration—require reinforcement through constant accusations—discoveries of ever more subtle, unconscious, or "micro" racist attacks. Racist incidents are sometimes even fabricated out of whole cloth.[260] These subjective and expanded accusations of racism generate bitterness, however, further reinforcing mutual suspicion, starting the cycle of accusation yet again.

---

259  Stanley Kurtz, "The Wannabe Oppressed," National Review Online, October 16, 2013, https://www.nationalreview.com/education-week/wannabe-oppressed-stanley-kurtz/; Stanley Kurtz, "Ecologism: The Campus Cult of Victimhood," Academic Questions, Spring 2014, https://www.nas.org/academic-questions/27/1/ecologism_the_campus_cult_of_victimhood

260  Jason L. Riley, "Hate Crime Hoaxes Are More Common Than You Think," The Wall Street Journal, June 25, 2019, https://www.wsj.com/articles/hate-crime-hoaxes-are-more-common-than-you-think-11561503352

# Wholly Oppressive

If we consider what actually happened at Stanford (and in the academy as a whole) over time, it follows along these lines. Few junior faculty volunteered to teach Stanford's multiculturalist substitute for Western Civ.[261] The content of the course remained scattered and incoherent; student interest was low; and the substitute requirement was eventually canceled as a result. Although an alternative course focused on non-Western cultures never quite gelled, radical faculty and students involved in deliberations over the new requirement pushed to transform it into something more like a freshman course in colonial oppression.[262] And instead of demanding a true requirement in non-Western cultures, Stanford's Rainbow Alliance quickly turned its efforts toward agitation for a campus speech code. Policing racist expression—defined broadly, to the point of unconstitutionality—was of greater interest than studying non-Western societies.[263] Oppression narratives and accusations of racism were the real preoccupation of the Stanford identity groups that sank Western Civ, not explorations of non-Western ways of life.

True, to the extent that opponents in 1988 conceded that there was anything admirable about the West, it was demanded that Egypt, the Muslim Middle East, and China be presented as key sources of that goodness. In support of this view, historically questionable claims were cited to the effect that Socrates, Herodotus, Pythagoras, and Solon had drawn their ideas from the African civilizations in and around Egypt.[264] Once the requirement was cut and concessions to Western virtue were no longer required, however, critics shifted to oppression. Now the West was evil—except when it didn't exist. The illusory nature of the West, at first affirmed through the Allardyce thesis, was later driven home via globalization theory, a more respectable development of those early claims that the founding ideas of the West were stolen from Egypt. None of this made consistent sense, except as a way of disposing of an irritant. The West could be excoriated, or dissolved, depending on the needs of the moment and the issue at hand.

---

261  Barchas, "Stanford After the Fall," p. 30.
262  Ibid., pp. 29-31.
263  Ibid., p. 32.
264  Bill King, "Don't Compromise on CUS Proposal, BSU Spokesman Says," Statements Delivered to the Meeting of the Faculty Senate on 4 February, 1988," *Minerva*, Volume 27, Issues 2-3, June 1989, pp. 299-303.

The course that virtually created American multiculturalism, "Culture, Ideas, and Values," (CIV) was cut about a decade later for incoherence and lack of student interest.[265] A series of ever-more inchoate and undemanding humanities requirements followed until, in February of 2016, the school's conservative paper, *The Stanford Review* sent a petition to the student body calling for undergraduates to hold a vote on restoring a Western Civilization requirement.[266] Although the petition swiftly garnered signatures, in the words of the *Review's* editor-in-chief, Harry Elliott, "all hell broke loose" within days of the campaign's announcement.[267] The original Stanford controversy had been resurrected nearly three decades later, burdened by both similarities to and differences from the earlier dispute.

Once again, racism charges were everywhere. This excerpt from a *cri de coeur* by Loralee Sepsey, a sophomore of Native American descent, conveys the flavor:

> When I first read your petition, I thought that it was too obviously harmful to garner any support…Then I went and looked at the number of people who signed it…186 and counting in just a few days. I felt sick. I felt like crying. I felt so hurt and betrayed that so many people, so many of my Stanford peers would support such a disgusting initiative. Because underneath all of your cheap rhetorical wrapping paper, there is racism. There is elitism, and classism, and hatred. Your words are filled with spite and supremacy and privilege…What you call "universal" isn't universal to those not of the mainstream Western culture…you know, somewhere deep down beneath your convoluted pseudo-intellectual jargon, that this proposal is wrong. I'm upset because after years and years of studying Western civilization in the United States public education system, a student like me would be subjected to two more quarters of being force-fed white glorification…I'm upset that you imply the same insidiously vitriolic rhetoric that was

---

265 Allison Schneider, "Stanford Revisits the Course That Set Off the Culture Wars," *The Chronicle of Higher Education*, May 9, 1997, https://www.chronicle.com/article/Stanford-Revisits-the-Course/76768; Thai, "The IHUM Epic"; Justin Lai, "The Death of Stanford's Humanities Core," *The Stanford Review*, March 14, 2015, https://stanfordreview.org/the-death-of-stanfords-humanities-core/

266 Stanford Review Editorial Board, "Update on the State of Western Civilization at Stanford," National Association of Scholars, May 2, 2016, https://www.nas.org/blogs/dicta/update_on_the_state_of_western_civilization_at_stanford

267 "Stanford Student: 'All hell broke loose' over Western Civilization courses," YouTube, April 21, 2016, https://www.youtube.com/watch?v=CsZQ48ApPRo

found in the debate over Indian boarding schools in the early 20th century—the argument that in order to succeed in this country, you need to be Westernized and assimilated. Kill the Indian, save the man.[268]

At first glance very little appears to have changed in three decades. The prospect of a new Western Civ requirement immediately reignited the old controversy. Sepsey's piece parallels Amanda Kemp's incendiary 1987 charge that Western Culture's real message was equivalent to an N-word insult. Yet Kemp had at least allowed that supporters of Western Culture may not have had a conscious racist motivation. Sepsey, by contrast, is certain that the *Review* holds bigoted intentions. One thing that hasn't changed is that in neither case are the racism charges softened by a willingness to include influential minority and female authors. Given three decades of dominance by the multicultural gospel, however, the right to label any challenge to the reigning orthodoxy as racist was now taken for granted.

No-one would have mistaken Stanford's 2016 donnybrook over Western Civ for a decorous college debate tournament. Accusations of bigotry, vicious unprintable insults, and threats of blacklisting were the order of the day. Signatories of the Western Civ petition were confronted with racism accusations in dorms, dining halls, and social media. According to reports, a student who'd published an anonymous op-ed in support of Western Civ was quickly unmasked and suspended from a leadership position in a supposedly apolitical low-income student advocacy group.[269]

In Elliott's view, the campus had fallen hostage to "threats of vengeance and ostracisation."[270] "The ability to have any reasonable discourse on this topic seems to have disappeared," he said.[271] Leaders of the multiculturalist faction, in contrast, were incredulous that

---

268 Loralee Sepsey, "You Remind Me of Carlisle," *The Stanford Arts Review*, February 27, 2016, http://stanfordartsreview.com/you-remind-me-of-carlisle-2/
269 Harry Elliott, "The Western Civilization Witch-Hunt," *The Stanford Review*, Winter 2016, https://stanfordreview.org/the-western-civilization-witch-hunt/; Jennifer Kabbany, "Stanford erupts in controversy after student petition calls for mandatory Western Civ classes," *The College Fix*, February 25, 2016, https://www.thecollegefix.com/stanford-erupts-controversy-student-petition-calls-mandatory-western-civ-classes/; Rachelle Peterson, "Stanford Students: Offering Western Civilization Classes Destroys Diversity," National Association of Scholars, April 8, 2016, https://www.nas.org/blogs/dicta/stanford_students_offering_western_civilization_classes_destroys_diversity; Joy Pullman, "Stanford Students Fight Campus Iconoclasts For Western Civilization," *The Federalist*, April 7, 2016, https://thefederalist.com/2016/04/07/stanford-students-fight-campus-iconoclasts-for-western-civilization/
270 Elliott, "Western Civilization Witch-Hunt."
271 Kabbany, "Stanford erupts."

restoration of Western Civ had been floated at all. Multiculturalists called the proposal "harmful to our campus well-being" and encouraged those troubled by the *Review's* petition to contact Stanford's Office of Counseling and Psychological Services.[272]

One of the sharpest student replies to the *Review's* proposal, penned by Erika Lynn, Abigail Persephone, and Joanna Kreeger, challenged the claim that Western culture had advanced global liberty, intellectual inquiry, and modern economic development:

> If you ask most people on the planet, they would be able to tell you from lived experience that the "developments" which came along with the invasion by Western civilizations did not equate to a basis for other freedoms: it in fact led to their relegation to the bottom of a system that tried to strip them of their culture, their land and their dignity. They would tell you that before the West colonized and occupied their land, they had different conceptions of life and liberty, which had served them well for the hundreds, if not thousands, of years prior to Western occupation... A Western Civilizations series would explicitly entrench the idea that the purpose of education is neither to critically question oppression, nor even to critically deal with the problems of our time. Rather, a Western Civ requirement would necessitate that our education be centered on upholding white supremacy, capitalism, and colonialism, and all other oppressive systems that flow from Western civilizations...[273]

How did Stanford's 2016 Western Civ debate compare to the controversy of 1987-88? Claims that the West is either an illusory construction or a byproduct of global influences played negligible roles in the revived dispute. And after a three-decade lapse in the course, it was no longer necessary to draw on Allardyce to bust the supposed myth of a venerable Western Civ teaching tradition. Thirty years of attacks had left the West in such bad odor with its critics that claiming global credit for

---

272 Jacob Nierenberg, "Stanford Review's Western Civilization proposal draws sharp reactions," *The Stanford Daily*, February 26, 2016, https://www.stanforddaily.com/2016/02/26/stanford-review-western-civilization-proposal-draws-sharp-reactions/; Sepsey, "You Remind Me of Carlisle."

273 Erika Lynn, Abigail Persephone, Joanna Kreeger, "The White Civ's Burden," *The Stanford Daily*, February 22, 2016, https://www.stanforddaily.com/2016/02/22/the-white-civs-burden/

the West's achievements was no longer desirable. The debate was dominated instead by "the left-wing perception that Western Civilization is wholly oppressive."[274]

## Who's Teaching Us?

Those attacks on Western Civ may seem to challenge this report's contention that multiculturalism has little to do with "culture." After all, the student critics cited above deny that Western ideals of liberty and equality appeal or apply universally. That is classic cultural relativism. Appearances to the contrary however, multiculturalists are not particularly relativist. Especially when it comes to social liberalism, multiculturalists are eager to impose Western individualist values on the world. Paradoxically, however, this moral certainty is driven by multiculturalism's inability to credit the reality of any tradition at all. Deconstructionist suspicion and progressive crusading are yoked together.

At the height of the 2016 Western Civ controversy, a coalition of activist groups at Stanford called "Who's Teaching Us" (WTU) issued a set of demands that served as a reply of sorts to the *Stanford Review's* Western Civ initiative.[275] This list included a demand that the next president and provost of Stanford "break the legacy of white leadership and cisgender male leadership" (i.e. should be a woman of color, or perhaps a transgender man of color); a demand that Stanford establish a system of anonymous reporting on faculty microaggressions to be used in professional evaluations (a likely violation of both free speech and academic freedom); and a demand that would almost certainly have reformed out of existence the last institutional redoubt of the Western canon on campus, the SLE program. A look at some of the other demands issued by the opponents of Western Civ in 2016 reveals the real ideology of these multiculturalists. "Culture" has little to do with it.

Consider the demand that Stanford's diversity course requirement "be reformed so that it only includes classes that address diversity as it relates to issues of power, privilege, and systems of oppression."

---

274 Stanford Review Editorial Board, "Update on the State of Western Civilization at Stanford."
275 Nierenberg, "Stanford Review's Western Civilization proposal draws sharp reactions;" The "Who's Teaching Us?" demands are posted at: https://pastebin.com/z51Ys0gN; Elliot Kaufman, Harry Elliott, "Who's Teaching Us, Unmasked," *The Stanford Review*, March 27, 2016, https://stanfordreview.org/whos-teaching-us-unmasked/

Multiculturalists are here demanding that courses on, say, the character and achievements of Chinese or African cultures actually be barred from inclusion in Stanford's diversity requirement. Not culture, per se, but themes of Western oppression and the need to resist it were the real focus of Stanford's campus activists in 2016.

Nor was this new. Recall that prior to CIV's collapse of its own incoherence in the 1990s there was talk among radical students and faculty of turning it into something closer to a requirement in colonial oppression.[276] That may not have been a politically achievable goal, yet the missing (if still limited) coherence of academic multiculturalism lies here. A singular focus on Western oppression is what the most determined and strategic advocates of "multiculturalism" have wanted all along, and this has little to do with "culture."

The demand for courses on "issues of power, privilege, and systems of oppression" is easily read as an effort to radicalize and politicize Stanford's diversity requirement. Yet those unfamiliar with the shifting currents of academe may miss the extent to which intellectual paradigms focused on systems of power and oppression are now antagonistic to the very idea of culture. It was noted above that Edward Said's *Orientalism*, the founding text of postcolonial theory, is a root and branch attack on the concept of culture itself. Said's core claim is that representations of the Other as culturally distinct are in fact subtle rationalizations of colonial domination. Drawing on Foucault, Said doubts that any real knowledge of cultural difference is possible. Instead Said rates so-called knowledge of others as a sly technique of "power." That is, history and anthropology are less accounts of the world than propaganda-sheets justifying the dominance of their authors. Allardyce uses this strategy as well, dismissing the reality of the Western tradition and treating apparent knowledge of its character and history as the ruse of a war-making elite.

Stanford's activist students in 2016 were thus effectively demanding the replacement of courses in cultural difference with courses grounded in Foucauldian, post-colonial, and neo-Marxist perspectives. The *Stanford Review* rightly characterized WTU's demands as a call for the creation of "a postcolonial criticism machine."[277]

---

276 "CIV" here is not "Western Civ" but "Culture, Ideas, and Values," the multicultural requirement that replaced Stanford's core "Western Culture" course.
277 Kaufman and Elliott, Who's Teaching Us, Unmasked."

As noted above, however, a key qualification is that even the most radical postcolonial theorists sometimes allow for "strategic essentialism." (For more on strategic essentialism, see Part Two of this report.) From this perspective, it is sometimes necessary to speak of marginalized races and ethnicities as if their communities and histories possessed more reality and continuity than postmodernists generally allow. This exception to the deconstructionist rule is granted as a way of supporting the resistance of "struggling groups" against oppressive power. Modern multiculturalists thus still do sometimes speak the language of cultural relativism and difference. Press that language a bit, however, and it melts away.

## Latinx

Consider yet another feature of the WTU manifesto. Throughout that document, WTU uses the word "Latinx" (pronounced: Lah-teen-ex) when referring to students or faculty who are more usually called "Hispanic" or "Latino." "Latinx" is a new word especially popular with American college students. The ideology behind its coinage is revealing.

"Latinx" is a gender-neutral variation of "Latino," a way of avoiding the masculine, inclusive plural "o" ending in a language built around gendered nouns. Rising to popularity with transgenderism and the LGBTQ+ movement, "Latinx" is embraced by those who strive to be "inclusive" and "non-binary" in matters of gender. That is, "Latinx" does not assume that everyone is either a heterosexual male or female. As one advocate puts it, Latinx "effectively de-naturalizes…hetero-cis-normativity, and challenges the androcentrism and unequal power relations embedded [in the word 'Latino.']"[278]

How did students seemingly bent on defending traditional cultures against the imperialist impositions of America and the West turn into advocates for a term as untraditional as "Latinx?" Answering that question yields insight into Stanford's decades-long battle over Western Civ, and provides a useful perspective on the "imaginary" character of history and culture as well.

The word "Latinx" appears to have been coined a couple of decades ago by Latino members of the LGBTQ+ community in the United

---

[278] Salvador Vidal-Ortiz, Juliana, Martinez, "Latinx thoughts: Latinidad with an X," *Latino Studies*, 2018, Volume 16, p. 393.

States.[279] Then, in December of 2014, a Mexican-American student group at Columbia University changed its name from Chicano Caucus to Chicanx Caucus. ("Chicano" denotes a person of Mexican descent.) This is appears to have set off a national trend of name changes among "Chicanx," but more often "Latinx," campus student groups.[280] In November of 2015, when student protests broke out nationwide following confrontations over race at Yale and the University of Missouri, the public began to notice the unfamiliar word "Latinx" in the lists of protesting student groups. Google searches on "Latinx" spiked and the term began to take root in progressive and academic circles.[281] While there is anecdotal evidence that "Latinx" and other x-ended terms are deployed by gender-activists in Latin America, the word is almost completely unknown among the vast majority of Spanish speakers outside of the United States.[282] "Latinx" is difficult for native Spanish speakers to pronounce, much less understand.

While American progressives generally favor the shift from "Latino" to "Latinx," a few on the left have made bold to reject this coinage. These recalcitrants condemn "Latinx" as the product of an elitist identity politics and an American linguistic imperialism that effectively erases the Spanish language and centuries of Latin American history, while disregarding the wishes of millions who feel that their identities as men or women are central to who they are, including many "queer constituencies." According to these critics, implicitly accusing the Spanish language of "patriarchy" and "toxic masculinity" is a typical act of U.S. neo-colonial arrogance, even if emanating in this case from

---

279  Cristobal Salinas Jr., Adele Lozano, "Mapping and recontextualizing the evolution of the term *Latinx*: An environmental scanning in higher education," *Journal of Latinos and Education*, 2017, p. 3.
280  Ibid., pp. 5-6.
281  Tanisha Love Ramirez, Zeba Blay, "Why People Are Using the Term 'Latinx,'" *Huffington Post*, July 5, 2016, https://www.huffpost.com/entry/why-people-are-using-the-term-latinx_n_57753328e4b0cc0fa136a159
282  Raul A. Reyes, "To Be Or Not To Be Latinx? For Some Hispanics, That Is the Question," NBC News, November 6, 2017, https://www.nbcnews.com/news/latino/be-latinx-or-not-be-latinx-some-hispanics-question-n817911; Steven Nuno-Perez, Gwen Aviles, "Is 'Latinx' elitist? Some push back at the word's growing use," NBC News, March 7, 2019, https://www.nbcnews.com/news/latino/latinx-elitist-some-push-back-word-s-growing-use-n957036; "Do Spanish people use the term Latinx to describe themselves or it's just an American English word?" Quora, December 30, 2017, https://www.quora.com/Do-Spanish-people-use-the-term-Latinx-to-describe-themselves-or-its-just-an-American-English-word

academic elites.[283] That critique from the left is condemned, in turn, by the even lefter-than-left as covertly sexist, heteronormative, and cisnormative.[284]

There is also a substantive reply from the gender radicals to charges of "linguistic imperialism." Proponents of "Latinx" say that Spanish itself is a colonizer language. Spain long ago wiped out pre-Columbian indigenous tongues, many of which did not have gendered nouns in the style of European Romance languages. Proponents of "Latinx" also note that the sexuality of indigenous South and Central Americans was very different than that of their Spanish colonizers. Some indigenous South and Central American groups are said to have recognized and accepted what are now called "third gender" categories (i.e. something similar to contemporary "non-binary" gender identities). The term "Latinx" is thus touted as a revival of indigenous, pre-Columbian sexuality. In this view, "Latinx" isn't Anglo-Imperialism at all. It's actually a belated indigenous rebellion against colonial European sexuality.[285]

This claim is part of a broader turn on the part of Latino college students in the United States toward identification with the pre-Columbian past. So, for example, the letter "x," used in a manner derived from the ancient Nahuatl word *Mexicano* (pronounced as "shh"), is often inserted into modern words to express identification with pre-Hispanic belief-systems and identities. For example, "Xicano" would be written instead of "Chicano."[286]

Yet the claim that Latinx-using American college students are rebelling against Spanish colonial values under the influence of pre-Columbian sexuality is a fantasy. Here is where postmodern notions like the "invention of tradition" and "imagined communities" really do apply. Of course culture is profoundly shaped by self-consciousness—by the collective identities we see ourselves as participating in—but not only by that. Proponents of "Latinx" and "Xicano" at elite universities are

---

283 Gilbert Guerra, Gilbert Orbea, "The argument against the use of the term 'Latinx,' " *The Phoenix: The independent newspaper of Swarthmore College*, November 19, 2015, https://swarthmorephoenix.com/2015/11/19/the-argument-against-the-use-of-the-term-latinx/; Hector Luis Alamo, "The X-ing of Language: The Case AGAINST 'Latinx,' " *Latino Rebels*, https://www.latinorebels.com/2015/12/12/the-x-ing-of-language-the-case-against-latinix/; Catalina (Kathleen) M. de Onis, "What's in an 'x'? An Exchange about the Politics of 'Latinx,' " *Chiricu Journal*, 2017, Vol. 1.2, pp. 78-91.
284 Maria R. Scharron-del Rio, Alan A. Aia, "The Case FOR 'Latinx': Why Intersectionality Is Not a Choice," *Latino Rebels*, December 5, 2015, https://www.latinorebels.com/2015/12/05/the-case-for-latinx-why-intersectionality-is-not-a-choice/; de Onis, "What's in an 'x'?"
285 Scharron-del Rio and Aia, "the Case FOR 'Latinx"; Salinas and Lozano, "Mapping and recontextualizing," p. 10.
286 Richard T. Rodriguez, "X marks the spot," *Cultural Dynamics*, 2017, Vol. 29(3), p. 207; Claudia Milian, "Extremely Latin, XOXO: Notes on LatinX," *Cultural Dynamics*, 2017, Vol. 29(3), p. 127.

culturally modern Americans and Westerners, whether they imagine themselves to be or not. The claim that they are restoring pre-Columbian sexuality is mere "strategic essentialism," the sort of claim that would be mercilessly skewered in academic journals were it not being made on behalf of an ethnic minority.

The term "Latinx" didn't emerge in Mexico—the land of the ancient Nahautl and the place where the indigenous Zapotec people still thrive. (The Zapotec are said to allow for "third gender" identities.)[287] "Latinx" rose to popularity in the United States as merely one in a series of terms—like "cisgender" and "heteronormativity"—deployed by young progressive Americans, the great majority of whom have no ethnic connection with Mexico or Latin America. All of these terms are part of a cultural-revolution run on intensely individualist principles. Such principles are characteristically developed first and most fully in the West, and particularly in the United States. This case is no different.

The underlying premise of contemporary gender theory is that biological sex is radically distinct from gender identity. Thus the individual ought to be free to choose his/her/hir own identity without taking into account either traditional sexual complementarity or the traditional procreative end of sexuality within the family. ("Hir" is one of the new gender-neutral pronouns suggested for English.) In this view, individuals ought to be free to construct any form of family desired, without fear of constraint from social expectations. If anything, society is obligated to recognize and support whatever form of gender-identity and family an individual may choose to construct.

Contemporary gender theory is thus a development or radicalization of classic American individualism. The modern, Western, and very American presuppositions that gave birth to "Latinx," "cisgender," and "hir," are alien to indigenous Latin American cultures, all of which tended to subordinate the individual to social expectations. And the understanding of human sexual and social nature that stands behind "Latinx" is particularly alien to the traditional Catholic faith, which has played an integral role in Latin American culture for the past several hundred years.

This point is almost never made in either the scholarly or general public debate over "Latinx," undoubtedly because it would swiftly

---

287 Salinas and Lozano, "Mapping and recontextualizing," p. 10.

ignite charges of bigotry and reaction. Those who condemn the "linguistic imperialism" of the term "Latinx" are instead at pains to stress that they do not object to the premises of modern gender theory.

Yet shouldn't we expect college students who insist that the individualist ways of the West are not universal to demur at the use of "Latinx?" Shouldn't we expect Stanford students to point to the Catholic traditions of Latin America and invoke Biblical phrases like, "male and female created he them," to oppose the adoption of gender-neutral terms? That, after all, would be the response from classic cultural relativism. Nothing could be more at odds with modern gender theory than traditional Catholic views of sexual complementarity, procreation, and the family. Yet students who employ cultural relativism to oppose a Western Civ requirement adopt "Latinx" with enthusiasm. As this report is being written, Stanford's Chicana/o-Latina/o Studies department is considering changing its name to Chicanx/Latinx Studies. And the main objection to that name change is not its affront to traditional Latin Catholic culture, but rather the potential de-radicalization and de-politicization of a term once associated with queer communities should "Latinx" become a label for cisgender students as well.[288] How can we explain this repudiation of "culture", given that "Latinx" does indeed appear to impose American individualist premises on Latin American language and tradition, the very sin for which supporters of WTU condemned the *Stanford Review*?

It would all make sense if Stanford's supposedly multicultural radicals were actually very modern American individualists. In that case, however, they ought to be reading John Locke. Anyone who's comfortable using "Latinx" is ready to explore the West's great books, and needs to do so in order to grasp what's at stake in the debates they care about most. Is the decline of traditional family norms a welcome advance of the Western individualist tradition, or a dangerous radicalization of it? Does the ethic of gender liberation free individuals from oppression, or undercut the virtue and community needed to balance our individualism out? Those questions and others can be answered more deeply through readings of the ancients, the great Christian thinkers, the founding theorists of liberalism, Marx, de Tocqueville, de Beauvoir, and more.

---

288   Rodríguez, "X marks the spot"; Nohemi Davila, "Chicana/o-Latina/o Studies department holds forum to discuss renaming," *The Stanford Daily*, May 10, 2018, https://www.stanforddaily.com/2018/05/10/chicanao-latinao-studies-department-holds-forum-to-discuss-renaming/; Rigoberto Marquéz, "What's in the 'x' of Latinx?" Center for Comparative Studies in Race & Ethnicity, July 9, 2018, https://medium.com/center-for-comparative-studies-in-race-and/whats-in-the-x-of-latinx-9266ed40766a

# Intersectionality

Yet another aspect of the "Latinx" controversy exposes and explains the minimal role that "culture" actually plays in so-called multiculturalism. Standing at the confluence of the gay and Latino movements, the term "Latinx" exemplifies the newly influential concept of "intersectionality."[289] Intersectionality theory holds that individuals embody multiple and interlocking forms of oppression that add up to more than the sum of each part. So a Latina woman, or better yet, a gender-fluid Latinx whose biological birth sex was female, would experience multiple forms of oppression, each of which would need to be understood in light of the others. That is the theory, at any rate. The best way to approach the "intersectionality" movement, however, is through its on-campus political practice.

In a 2018 essay for *Commentary*, Elliot Kaufman, formerly an editor of the *Stanford Review*, powerfully laid out the dynamics of Stanford's intersectional politics.[290] (Elliot Kaufman is not to be confused with the *Review's* former editor-in-chief Harry Elliott, discussed above.) Student politics at Stanford has been dominated since 2009, says Kaufman, by a highly organized "intersectional" coalition of minority groups, joined by a number of white "allies." The coalition Kaufman describes is obviously descended from the Rainbow Alliance that cancelled the Western Culture requirement three decades ago. It now rules Stanford unchallenged.

Stanford's intersectional coalition defines itself as a collection of "marginalized" groups allying out of a sympathy born of shared oppression. This coalition of the marginalized conceives of itself as standing in opposition to a global "power structure" whose machinations are fairly homogeneous, even when going under different names. So, for example, "Stanford Out of Occupied Palestine," an intersectional coalition made up of 19 largely minority-based student organizations, calls on the university to divest from Israel. This group charges Israel with 1) training U.S. police to "deal with black people the way its occupation forces deal with Palestinians"; 2) permitting religious discrimination against gays; and 3) giving technical advice to U.S. immigration enforcement

---

289 Salinas and Lozano, "Mapping and recontextualizing," pp. 1-2.
290 Elliot Kaufman, "The Campus Intersectionality Craze," *Commentary*, May 2018, https://www.commentary-magazine.com/articles/campus-intersectionality-craze/

officials based on Israel's experiences with its border wall. So the intersectional coalition of the marginal is unified by resistance to what it sees as a fairly monolithic alliance of "oppressive power."

The dominant force within Stanford's intersectional alliance is the Students of Color Coalition (SOCC). Each year, SOCC endorses about a dozen candidates for student council, requiring them to campaign as a slate in exchange. The effect, says Kaufman, is to prevent candidates from building independent profiles, rendering them subordinate to the larger machine. SOCC candidates have won control of the student counsel every year since 2009.

According to Kaufman, the result is that individual minority students at Stanford have very little scope for independence from the intersectional alliance. Having left friends and family for the first time, Stanford freshmen find that ethnic and racial identity groups provide "soft social landing spots with peers from similar backgrounds." The downside of the social home provided by campus identity groups is that breaking with intersectional orthodoxy on any given issue triggers social ostracism. When, for example, a leftist Latina member of the student council declined to support divestment from Israel, threats of ostracism swiftly forced her to reverse her vote. Any break from the intersectional menu of issues is understood as a treacherous abandonment of the marginalized in the service of oppressive power.

As a campus conservative affiliated with the *Stanford Review*, Kaufman is no friend of the intersectional alliance. Yet consider the following characterization of Stanford's political scene by Professor Larry Diamond, a moderate liberal inclined to give his school the benefit of the doubt:

> A lot of students involved in identity issues tend to be more politically active than others and they're better organized. They are seen by many of their peers to be at the center of the moral universe here, and to oppose them is to feel kind of retrograde. Many faculty members feel that they have to tread very carefully when discussing these [identity-related] issues.[291]

---

291   Richard Bernstein, "Culture War and Peace at Stanford: The PC Uprising 25 Years On," *RealClearInvestigations*, April 5, 2019, https://www.realclearinvestigations.com/articles/2019/04/03/culture_war_and_peace_at_stanford.html

Although Diamond is less critical of Stanford than Kaufman, the broader pictures they paint closely match.

Intersectional alliances of the "marginalized" now typically hold the political initiative at elite universities, while the moderate-liberal majority tends to sit disengaged on the sidelines.[292] Unwilling to appear supportive of the alleged oppressors against the putatively oppressed, moderately liberal students and faculty seldom challenge the multicultural alliance. Minorities who break ranks with intersectional orthodoxy are granted even less toleration.

The *Stanford Review's* campaign to restore a Western Civ requirement was ultimately rejected by a 6-1 margin in a 2016 vote of the undergraduate student body. The *Review's* proposal faced not only heated opposition from the multicultural/intersectional coalition, but a lack of support from Stanford students more focused on STEM studies than humanities.[293] These are the sort of students the Western Civ requirement was originally designed to round out. That only worked, however, when the course was imposed on reluctant future doctors, scientists, and engineers by the faculty. A student-initiated restoration of Western Civ was always a noble but quixotic quest.

A bit of reflection shows that campus intersectional politics tends to strip the "culture" out of multiculturalism. What Latino on an elite college campus would dare challenge the shift to "Latinx" on the grounds of his Catholic faith or tradition? Who would dare invoke sexual complementarity and its role in *familismo* (family unity) to argue against the x?

With "marginalization" as the intersectional coalition's unifying principle, the actual content of its divergent cultural components can only endanger the alliance's strength. The more Catholic the Latinos, the more Muslim the Muslims, and the more gay the gays, the less would these groups have in common. A Catholic-identified Latina might be reluctant to advocate for divestment from Israel, for example, certainly more reluctant than a Muslim member of Students for Justice in Palestine.

Yet the intersectional alliance only wins when everyone stays on board. Keeping members in line thus demands a least-common-denominator approach in which "marginalization" and resistance to "power" become the passports to identity. Your place in the clash between

---

292  Benjamin Ginsberg, *The Fall of the Faculty: The Rise of the All-Administrative University and Why It Matters*, (Oxford: Oxford University Press, 2011), pp. 97-102.
293  Stanford Review Editorial Board, "Update on the State of Western Civilization at Stanford."

the powerful and the oppressed is what makes you intersectional. Everything else is a distraction. The "cultural" components of the coalition are thus important only insofar as they influence the quotient of relative oppression or privilege, not for their actual content.

All this drives the intersectional alliance to downplay culture and accentuate race. Race becomes the sign of shared oppression and essentially replaces culture at the core of modern intersectional identity. Latino students and students of Middle-Eastern Muslim descent are associated with very different and potentially clashing cultures. Their skins tones are similar, however. Accusations of racism thus unify the coalition in a way that charges of cultural insensitivity cannot. The key marker of intersectional identity is thus "people of color," an insight affirmed by the name of the dominant force within Stanford's intersectional alliance, the "Students of Color Coalition."

Recall that one of the key demands of "Who's Teaching Us?" was the removal of courses that address culture alone from Stanford's diversity requirement. Only "classes that address diversity as it relates to issues of power, privilege, and systems of oppression" should qualify, said WTU. Another plank of WTU's manifesto ran as follows:

> WE DEMAND alternative Integrated Learning Environments (ILE) humanities and writing programs be developed that center social justice and anti-oppression scholarship, with an emphasis on works by people of color and PoC frameworks.

So campus intersectionality drives culture out and replaces it with an oppression-based worldview centered on race—on "People of Color frameworks." With traditional cultural differences hollowed out, accusations of racism become the only available route to group identity, cohesion, and political success.

## Insufficiently Authentic

If intersectionality tends to strip students of their distinctive cultural traditions, resistance is apparently slight. By the time students get to elite universities like Stanford, they are American individualists in good standing—often more so than they'd like to acknowledge. Already considerably distanced from their heritage cultures by American education, assimilation, and the pervasive power of pop culture, these students find politicized racial identities to be the quickest route to a sense of belonging at school.

Consider a study of "race-related stress" among Latino students during freshman year at a "predominantly white, highly selective institution."[294] This 2005 study, published by J. Derek Lopez in the *Journal of Hispanic Higher Education*, is very likely about freshman Latinos at Stanford. The undergraduate enrollment figures and the ethnic breakdown of the student body at the unnamed "highly selective, private university on the West Coast" examined by Lopez closely matches the student population and demographics of Stanford.[295] Stanford has long boasted an unusually diverse student body, and it's difficult to find another "highly selective private university on the West Coast" with minority demographics that resemble Stanford's. Additionally, like Stanford, Lopez's target school runs on a quarterly rather than a semester system. If by some chance Lopez examined freshman Latinos at a different highly selective West Coast school with essentially identical demographics to Stanford, the lessons of his study would surely be relevant to Stanford.

After administering detailed surveys early in the first quarter and again at the beginning of the third quarter, Lopez found that Latino freshmen report very little racism at first, but significantly more discrimination later in the year. The big personal concerns as Latino students enter school are worries about their capacity to do the work, along with what Lopez and a small but growing scholarly literature call "intragroup marginalization" (criticism or shunning of group members judged insufficiently authentic or loyal by their racial, ethnic, or religious peers). By the end of freshman year, however, intragroup marginalization recedes as an issue and complaints about racism and a general sense of racial alienation become prominent instead.

Lopez takes these findings to mean that Latino freshmen are driven into balkanization by pervasive campus racism. His main evidence

---

294  J. Derek Lopez, "Race-Related Stress and Sociocultural Orientation Among Latino Students During Their Transition Into a Predominantly White, Highly Selective Institution," *Journal of Hispanic Higher Education*, Vol. 4, No. 4, October 2005, pp. 354-365.

295  There is some ambiguity about whether Lopez's study of "the entering class of 2000" refers to the class that entered Stanford in 2000 or the class scheduled to graduate in 2000. In any case, the undergraduate demographics of Stanford in 1997, 2000, and 2001 all closely match the demographics of the freshman class described by Lopez. See Lopez, "Race-Related Stress," pp. 355-356; Stanford Facts for 1997, p. 39, https://stacks.stanford.edu/file/druid:xh107dn5690/StanfordFacts_1997.pdf; Stanford Facts for 2000, p. 18, https://stacks.stanford.edu/file/druid:xh107dn5690/StanfordFacts_2000.pdf; Stanford Facts for 2001, p. 19, https://stacks.stanford.edu/file/druid:xh107dn5690/StanfordFacts_2001.pdf

of that racism consists of complaints by Latino freshmen that others expect them to perform poorly in class on account of their race. Lopez attributes these reports to racist suspicions on the part of white students that minorities have been admitted through affirmative action. But expectations of Latino underachievement, if they do exist among white students, could reflect awareness of racial preferences in admissions, and needn't indicate irrational prejudice or belief in the inherent inferiority of Latinos in general.

The literature on the "mismatch" effect offers a perfectly plausible alternative explanation for Lopez's data.[296] Studies of mismatch show that minority students at highly selective schools are often granted very large admissions preferences. These preferences effectively set minorities up for competition with classmates who are, in fact, far stronger academically. Affirmative action itself thus often leads to poor academic performance in courses that beneficiaries could have managed more adeptly at schools better matched to their academic preparation.

Unfortunately, highly selective schools keep the size of their minority admissions preferences secret, thereby misleading beneficiaries into believing that they are well-qualified to compete with peers who are in reality stronger academically. The result is often the withdrawal by minorities into racial enclaves where grievances against the school's alleged racism are nursed. Admissions preferences thus effectively set up their supposed beneficiaries for failure, while encouraging the assumption that most minorities on campus are there primarily because of preferences. In many cases that assumption is true.

The mismatch thesis is at least as plausible an explanation for Lopez's data as his own. But the aspect of Lopez's research of special interest here is "intracultural marginalization," by which Latino students fear alienation from their own ethnic group. The freshmen in Lopez's study began the year concerned about "pressures from my race on how to act or what to believe;" "pressures to show loyalty to my race;" and "people close to me thinking I am acting White." By the end of the

---

296 Peter Arcidiacono, Esteban Aucejo, Ken Spenner, "What Happens After Enrollment? An analysis of the time path in racial differences in GPA and major choice," *IZA Journal of Labor Economics*, 1, no. 5 (October 2012); Gail Heriot, "The Sad Irony of Affirmative Action," *National Affairs*, Winter 2013, https://www.nationalaffairs.com/publications/detail/the-sad-irony-of-affirmative-action; Heather MacDonald, *The Diversity Delusion: How Race and Gender Pandering Corrupt the University and Undermine Our Culture*, (New York: St. Martin's Press, 2018), pp. 53-59; Richard Sander, Stuart Taylor, Jr., *Mismatch: How Affirmative Action Hurts Students It's Intended to Help, And Why Universities Won't Admit It*, (New York: Basic Books, 2012); Stuart Taylor, "A Little-Understood Engine of Campus Unrest: Racial Admissions Preferences," *The American Spectator*, November 23, 2015, https://spectator.org/64739_little-understood-engine-campus-unrest-racial-admissions-preferences/

year, these concerns had receded, to be replaced by group solidarity and an accompanying conviction that the campus is racist. For Lopez, it's obvious that racial hostility is driving Latinos together. But his own data indicate there may be a better explanation.

Many Latino students entering this very Stanford-like school seem to be good candidates for intragroup marginalization. Fifty-seven percent of the freshman Latinos in this study attended high schools with a predominantly white student body. Lopez suggests that "the lack of exposure to other Latino students prior to matriculation" may explain the high initial levels of intragroup marginalization. Sixty-seven percent of freshmen Latinos in Lopez's study were middle-class, upper-middle-class, or upper class, with the remainder either poor or working-class. These relatively well-off students from predominantly white high-schools may at first have seemed poor fits for Latino identity politics.

Here we're reminded of the Edward Said effect, in which a young man raised as a Christian and forbidden to speak Arabic finished his schooling in America and avoided the company of Middle Eastern immigrants because he had so little in common with them. Said found his Middle-Eastern identity only belatedly, and through politics, not culture—through the creation of a worldview in which anti-Muslim bigotry appears to be everywhere, even in seemingly admiring studies of Middle Eastern culture, and indeed in the very idea of culture itself. It is possible that Latino freshmen at Stanford, perhaps already thrown off their stride by mismatch, discovered that oppression-based racial politics offers an easy route to ethnic credibility for the otherwise well-assimilated. Certainly, economically-comfortable, English dominant Latinos thoroughly at home with the culture of progressive American millennials would be the first to sign up for a term like "Latinx," or for a course in Saidian post-colonial theory. They'd need to keep finding racism everywhere, too. Without the racism charges, after all, their ticket to ride on the intersectional express might expire.

The Lopez study's stress on intragroup marginalization tallies with Harry Elliott's description of the 2016 battle over Stanford's Western Civ requirement, and with Elliott Kaufman's 2018 account of Stanford's intersectional coalition. Both highlight threats of social ostracism against minority students who break with the rainbow alliance. Yet Lopez's 2005 study predates the consolidation of intersectional political power in 2009. After 2009, pressures were likely added for conformity with demands from multiple groups within the coalition. With the consolidation of intersectional power, a Latino student might be criticized for, say, preferring "Latino" to "Latinx." This would be something closer to a repudiation of cultural tradition than its affirmation.

## Closed Mind

We are now in a position to draw together the primary threads of this report, namely: deconstructionist history's exaggerated and incoherent skepticism about the reality of national, cultural, and civilizational continuity; the moral certainties of campus intersectionality at institutions where relativism and historicism predominate; and the transformation of "expanded" charges of bigotry and racism from campus curiosities into central sources of contention in our national debates.

Assessing the three-decade legacy of Stanford's Western Culture debate in light of political philosopher and classicist Allan Bloom's nearly contemporaneous book *The Closing of the American Mind* (1987) helps us puzzle out changes in the academy since the Stanford battle. When the *Wall Street Journal* published a controversial syllabus from Stanford's new multicultural humanities requirement in 1989, Bloom hammered it in the paper and claimed vindication (as we saw in Part Two of this report). So Bloom's book is both a synoptic critique of the academy published at the time of the Stanford controversy, and a major point of contention in the battle itself.

Bloom's book opens with this observation: "There is one thing a professor can be absolutely certain of: almost every student entering the university believes, or says he believes, that truth is relative."[297] This, according to Bloom, is what has closed America's mind. Openness to everything turns the principle of individual natural rights at the heart of the American experiment into just another opinion. How about "openness" to Southern segregation? Or to Hindu widow burning?, asks Bloom. Since the search for truth is the fulcrum of liberal education, relativist openness undercuts the university as well. Why bother interrogating the truths of Western liberalism—or its alternatives—if the best you can ever come up with is just another ungrounded opinion? Doctrinaire "openness" actually shuts down serious thought.

Bloom's insight remains pertinent. We've discovered, after all, that Stanford students talk a good relativist game, but practice

---

297 Bloom, *Closing*, p. 25.

Western-individualist "cultural imperialism" instead. That inconsistency is not new. Notice the phrase, "or says he believes," in Bloom's opening formula. Students hold relativism less as a theoretical insight than as a moral prejudice, says Bloom. They cannot explain or defend it. Faced with the problem of Hindu widow-burning, "they either remain silent or reply that the British should never have been there in the first place."[298] Course requirements in non-Western cultures, Bloom maintains, do little to convey the actual content of other traditions, much less examine them critically. The point instead is to break our confidence in the West's standards, thereby upending the authority of standards altogether. "Let us be whatever we want to be," is the moral that campus relativists seek to impart. Campus relativism, then, is less a serious philosophical position than a roundabout way of promoting a radicalized brand of Western individualism.[299]

"Latinx" is today's version of Western individualist "imperialism;" in Bloom's day, student devotion to Third World development checked that box.[300] Even in the 1980s, determination to make "them" more like "us" lay buried beneath reflexive campus relativism. So students are relativists now in much the same doctrinaire yet thoroughly inconsistent way that students were relativists then.

The insistence of Stanford's "Who's Teaching Us?" coalition that courses with merely cultural content be dropped from Stanford's diversity requirement seems like a break from early-stage multiculturalism, however. If diversity requirements in Bloom's day were thin on the actual workings of non-Western cultures, the moral of those courses was clear: let a hundred flowers bloom, cultures and individuals alike must be free to live as they choose. The lesson of WTU's proposed 2016 diversity requirement change is different: the West's oppression of people of color must be featured, and recompensed by radical social transformation. It is true that soon after the Western Culture course was swept away, Stanford's radicals started plumping for something like a requirement in colonial oppression. But that push came largely during closed-door committee maneuvering. Now all-oppression all-the-time is a very public and prominent demand.

Calls for courses that teach the evils of the West—and nothing but the evils of the West—certainly resonate with the politics of today. Things

---

298  Ibid., p. 26.
299  Ibid., p. 41.
300  Ibid., p. 34.

were different in Bloom's time. *Closing* appeared at the end of the Reagan era, a period of relative calm on campus. Bloom worried that relativism had unstrung his students' yearning for truth, and thus for education itself. The students Bloom described were largely apolitical.[301] They were focused on themselves, not political crusades, yet another consequence of their declining confidence in truth. Today, on the other hand, the intersectional coalition's dominance presses everyone on campus to choose between alliance and opposition. In contrast to the apathetic eighties, politics is everywhere. Silent acquiescence or resentment from relatively apolitical students doesn't change that.

A couple of decades before the apathetic eighties, however, Bloom had seen worse. *Closing* concludes with a harrowing retrospective on Bloom's time at Cornell in 1969, when gun-toting members of the Afro-American Society occupied the administration building and used threats of violence to cow the faculty into submission.[302] Not the Reagan era but the tumultuous 1960s supply the real source and precedent for today's politicized campus. Bloom knew all about questionable accusations of racism tossed off to achieve political ends during the sixties. The racism charge was "a qualification equivalent to heretic in earlier times," and subject to like abuse, he maintained.[303] Bloom's Cornell experience also familiarized him with demands for courses focused on racism and oppression. *Closing* warned that with the collapse of confidence in truth, the tyrannical currents of sixties radicalism—and of a much older German student fascism—were destined to reemerge.[304]

## Random Atoms

So the question is how we got from the relative apathy of Bloom's 1980s to today's resurgence of sixties-descended radicalism. At least in broad strokes, Bloom warned that a new wave of campus intolerance was on the way. His treatment of the growing individualism of the 1980s may offer the best explanation of how the academy shifted from the radical sixties, to the apathetic eighties, and back again to the "woke" revolution of our time.

---
301 Ibid., p. 85.
302 Ibid., pp. 313-320.
303 Ibid., p. 318.
304 Ibid., pp. 309-315.

We think of the Reagan era as conservatism's moment of triumph, social conservativism included. After all, religious associations like the Moral Majority were highly influential at the time. Yet writing toward the end of Reagan's second term, Bloom described an America whose core institutions had in fact been hollowed out. "Country, religion, family, ideas of civilization....have been rationalized and have lost their compelling force. America is experienced not as a common project but as a framework within which people are only individuals....The advanced Left talks about self-fulfillment; the Right, in its most popular form, is Libertarian...."[305] Even the Moral Majority was on the defensive by the late 1980s, closing down shortly after the appearance of Bloom's book.[306] The denizens of elite universities, said Bloom, are now:

> "...free to decide whether they will believe in God or be atheists, or leave their options open by being agnostic; whether they will be straight or gay, or keep their options open; whether they will marry and whether they will stay married; whether they will have children—and so on endlessly. There is no necessity, no morality, no social pressure, no sacrifice...."[307]

Bloom is so prescient here that it's tempting to knock him for jumping the gun. How frayed were things, really, in 1987? Gay, straight, or keep their options open? Just wait till LGBTQ+ comes along. Neither believers nor atheists in 1987 could have imagined that in two short decades the number of "nones" responding to surveys on religious belief would match the number of Catholics or evangelicals.[308] As for marriage and children, delayed millennial marriage, declining birth rates, growing numbers of "families" consisting of one, and a big chunk of millennials who "always feel lonely" might have surprised even those warning of family decline in the eighties[309]

---

305  Ibid., p. 85.
306  Encyclopedia Britannica, "Moral Majority," https://www.britannica.com/topic/Moral-Majority
307  Bloom, *Closing*, p. 87.
308  Mark Movsesian, "The Devout and the Nones," *First Things*, April 22, 2019, https://www.firstthings.com/web-exclusives/2019/04/the-devout-and-the-nones
309  The Editorial Board, "America's Millennial Baby Bust," *The Wall Street Journal*, May 28, 2019, https://www.wsj.com/articles/americas-millennial-baby-bust-11559086198; Pew Research Center, "Millennials are less likely to be married than previous generations at the same age," https://www.pewsocialtrends.org/essay/millennial-life-how-young-adulthood-today-compares-with-prior-generations/psdt_02-14-19_generations-00-06/; YouGov, "Millennials are the loneliest generation," July 30, 2019, https://today.yougov.com/topics/lifestyle/articles-reports/2019/07/30/loneliness-friendship-new-friends-poll-survey

Homing in on elite students, Bloom was able to see America's across-the-board institutional decline well before it had fully played out. Like Wile E. Coyote chasing the Road Runner off a cliff, holding in mid-air and looking down just before his descent, Bloom was among the first to spy the bottom of the canyon.

The removal of social pressure had left Bloom's students in an oddly dissatisfied state, a feeling of "groundlessness," he called it.[310] Students were free to choose any life path, any lover, any friend, yet lacked any compelling reason for doing so. Without community, morality, or convention, life was reduced to directionless whim. Bloom's students yearned for more, yet social and moral reconstruction seemed beyond reach. Although the sixties were over, students were nostalgic for an era when people had actually believed in something. The prospect of getting drafted to fight in Vietnam was truly frightening. Yet nothing like that threatened students in the 1980s.[311]

Bloom fingered family decline as the mainspring of the new individualism, evident above all in the rising frequency of divorce.[312] The family is a keystone institution. Love of country, church, and community are encouraged by the nurture they offer to families. You're loyal to institutions because they care for you and yours. Remove the family linchpin and the wheel flies off the axle. Divorce, in particular, from the child's point of view, is a denial of unconditional love. In the absence of a family that directs and demands, yet also provides for and sacrifices unconditionally, reciprocal obligation and sacrifice on the part of the new generation makes no sense.

The result of family decline was a radical intensification of the problem of individualism first identified by Tocqueville. Individuals cut loose from community are reduced to random atoms floating through time. Tocqueville speaks of the way in which a man without either land, or a family tradition for whose continuation he is responsible, would come to feel but an aimless point in a meaningless flux.[313] That was in the 1830s, when America's robust families lacked only the long memories of aristocratic European houses. How much less would felt-continuity thrive in an America where many families last not a single generation? A land of broken families is primed to dismiss national, cultural, and civilizational traditions as dangerous illusions perpetrated by elites

---
310   Bloom, *Closing*, p. 109.
311   Ibid., p. 83.
312   Ibid., pp. 109-121.
313   Ibid., p. 84.

determined to exploit their sons for selfish ends (i.e. the Allardyce thesis). It was as a defense against this experience of isolation and "groundlessness" that recovering a sense of moral direction became a feature of the post-Bloom years.

## No Melt

Race has stepped into the void, playing perhaps the pivotal role. The student ethos of the eighties as described by Bloom was a triumph of equality.[314] Ancient religious, national, and ethnic differences had simply ceased to matter, with the notable exception of race. "Just at the moment when everyone else has become 'a person,'" said Bloom, "blacks have become blacks."[315]

This was not the result of invidious discrimination. On the contrary, Bloom maintained that campus race-consciousness was created by the silent and drastic lowering of admissions standards for many blacks. Unprepared students would now inevitably fail in large numbers, or would have to be passed without having learned. Black students were thus made to feel as though their abilities were under constant suspicion. In effect, the beneficiaries of preferences had been set up for shame or failure by administrative manipulation.[316] Bloom was laying out the "mismatch" theory long before scholarship on the phenomenon had emerged.

It took radical racial politics to extract minorities from this trap. The manufacture of racial grievances saved them from the impossible dilemma they'd been saddled with by the misplaced racial guilt of administrators. Universities aren't teaching truth, it was now claimed, just the myths required to support the system of domination. If some black students perform poorly, it is merely because they've been forced to imitate white culture and conform to its standards. For many minority students, this uneasy combination of relativism and Marxism seemed to explain their daunting challenges. The logical outcome of the new ideology was separatism in dorms, coursework, and much else. The black experience became the focus of study, thus curtailing awkward contacts and comparisons with other students. What scholars now

---

314  Ibid., pp. 88-91.
315  Ibid., p. 72.
316  Ibid., pp. 91-97.

call "intragroup marginalization" grew proportionally in importance as well. Bloom reported that the pressures on middle and upper-class blacks to socialize along racial lines and adopt a radical political stance had changed the behavior of many.[317] (This story is told for another elite university by Dion Pierre and Peter Wood in an NAS report entitled, *Neo-Segregation at Yale*.)[318] And Bloom's account is perfectly consistent with the 2000 Lopez study of Latinos at Stanford (or a very Stanford-like university), and with Kaufman's report on today's intra-minority pressures within Stanford's intersectional coalition.

As in the other cases examined here, the apparent relativism of black students in the eighties was thin and contradictory, more a debaters' point than a serious program of cultural separatism. Black students, according to Bloom, participated fully in the common American culture; but were "doing it by themselves." The result was a near-constant emphasis on alleged racism. In the absence of sufficient cultural differences, expanded accusations of racism were the only remaining justification for de facto racial separatism on campus.

Bloom's final assessment was pessimistic. He feared that the knock-on effects of preferences would trigger "a long-term deterioration of the relations between the races in America." Yet he never expected what he viewed as the exceptional case of race to become the new rule. He knew that racial conflict would persist, but did not anticipate that it would expand into the central line of fracture—or the central source of meaning—in society at large.

Bloom is rightly credited for foreseeing that something like Stanford's Western Culture controversy would emerge. The Stanford conflict bore out his claim that confidence in the Western liberal tradition had waned and been replaced by a strangely inconsistent relativism. Yet Bloom's prescience disguises the extent to which the forces driving the Stanford controversy were at least somewhat at odds with his overall picture. Bloom saw race as the great exception. Like others at the time, he assumed that every other identity would "melt."

We've seen, however, that Stanford's Western Culture controversy was driven by a Rainbow Alliance of blacks, Latinos, Asians, Native Americans, and leftist whites. Stanford's demographics were unusual at the time, different from what Bloom had seen among his students at

---

317  Ibid., pp. 91-97.
318  Dion Pierre, Peter Wood, *Neo-Segregation at Yale: Part of Separate But Equal, Again: Neo-Segregation in American Higher Education*, (New York: National Association of Scholars, 2019), https://www.nas.org/blogs/dicta/separate_but_equal_again_neo_segregation_at_yale

Cornell or the University of Chicago. Since then, greatly increased immigration from South and Central America and from Muslim-majority and other non-Western countries as well, in conjunction with continued preferences, has turned the demographics of the American academy at large into something resembling the composition of Stanford in 1987. University Latinos are now subject to preference-driven dynamics that resemble what Bloom described thirty years ago for blacks. Meanwhile, the practice of alliance politics has delivered de facto control of universities to the intersectional coalition. Access to political power has rendered a radical political stance that much more attractive.

## Moral Minimalism

More importantly, radical racial politics now fill a gap that other moral possibilities cannot. Hearing today's passionate denunciations of America's allegedly systemic racism, it's easy to conclude that the old relativism has been abandoned for a return to moral certainty. That is too simple a take. The old moralities have not been restored, nor has the veneer of incoherent post-sixties relativism disappeared. Classic cultural relativism was evident in the student attacks on the 2016 proposal to restore Western Civ at Stanford, and nihilist-tinged Foucauldian post-colonialism pervades the courses favored by Stanford's radicals. These intellectual currents continue to coexist inconsistently with outrage at the insult to individual rights perpetrated by our putatively racist system.

The racism charge is powerful because Americans almost universally share the classically liberal presupposition that human beings are by nature free and equal individuals. To judge a person by the color of his skin rather than the content of his character, or to assume that races are unequal, outrages our classically liberal souls. Yet the relativists and postmodernists who dominate the academy disdain and debunk the presuppositions of classical liberalism as ethnocentric illusions or ruses of the powerful, even as they depend upon our classically liberal sensibilities to fuel outrage at these supposed manipulations and illusions.

Relativists dismiss the idea of individual rights as a Western prejudice, yet their attitude toward the multiplicity of cultures is actually a variation on classical liberalism: everyone is entitled to his own convictions, entire societies included. Although this relativist rule breaks with liberal individualism, at root it is an attempt to expand rights-based thinking to groups. So relativism is an outgrowth of liberal tolerance that simultaneously undermines and depends upon a classically liberal sensibility.

Postmodernism is similarly divided against itself. As we saw in the second part of this report, Foucault rejects the idea of "truth." For him, so-called truth is less a statement about reality than a way of looking at the world that legitimates and reinforces the powers that be. Classical liberalism, for Foucault, is thus not a claim about natural human equality, liberty, or individuality, but a worldview designed to solidify the position of the West's ruling elites. When students shout-down campus speakers with the claim that freedom of speech is a tool of white supremacy, they are making a Foucauldian point.[319]

In offering his argument, however, Foucault himself is staking a claim about what is true, and depending as well upon our "liberal" outrage at the inequalities supposedly supported by knowledge-systems like classical liberalism. So Foucauldian postmodernism contradicts and undermines the classically liberal convictions upon which outrage at racism depends, even as it quietly depends for its effect upon an appeal to our classically liberal sensibilities.

The new generation's faith in America's collective institutions has thus not been restored. Those institutions are tattered, and the academy's dominant ideologies treat the intellectual foundations upon which America's institutions rest as oppressive illusions. Even "culture" has proven unworkable as a fallback, since our radical individualism undermines non-Western cultures every bit as much as it undermines our own. That makes race the last best issue for those who believe in nothing else. That racism is wrong is the bare minimum we can all agree upon. Nowadays we find it difficult even to affirm, much less build upon, the classically liberal sensibility that we still reflexively hold. Since we collectively assent to little else, perpetual racial outrage over a relentlessly expanding target list is the last remaining path to meaning and power.

In his chapter on the sixties, Bloom anatomized the fundamental moral shift of that era. Sacrifice is the sine qua non of traditional morality. Civilizations, faith-communities, nations, and families care

---

319   Robby Soave, "Black Lives Matter Students Shut Down the ACLU's Campus Free Speech Event Because 'Liberalism is White Supremacy,'" Reason.com, October 4, 2017, https://reason.com/2017/10/04/black-lives-matter-students-shut-down-th/

for their members, while individuals sacrifice their immediate desires and interests for the greater good. Morality took a different path during the sixties by turning histrionic. As Bloom put it, "Thomas More's resistance to a tyrant's commands was the daily fare of students' imagination." Today, denizens of America's famously liberal campuses imagine themselves facing down Bull Connor in Birmingham on a daily basis. In practice, however, the new Bull Connor is just an old statue, considerably less of a threat than the original.

What comes off as moral intensity is moral minimalism instead. If requiring Plato or Aristotle, opposing Medicare for all, or refusing to fund universal "free" college education is not equivalent to Bull Connor's attack dogs, a moral charge sufficient to counter an otherwise groundless existence is lost. The frequency of the charges has to rise as the actual threat to well-being recedes. Minimalist definitions of morality—"racism and genocide are bad"—cannot keep groundlessness at bay unless racism and genocide turn up everywhere and often. Nowadays, they are omnipresent.

## Bordering on Hysteria

So students haven't exchanged relativism for the old morality. On the contrary, as the family decomposes and individualism continues to radicalize, the moral minimalism of averting racism and mass death are the sole remaining ethical imperatives.[320] The only collective action that even radical individualists can embrace with enthusiasm is a crusade to secure and advance individual rights. Fighting racism fits the bill, as does averting mass death from a climate apocalypse. (For more on the invention of new moral causes to fill the space vacated by the old Western Civ requirements, see Peter Wood's and Michael Toscano's NAS report, *What Does Bowdoin Teach?*)[321]

Maintaining the new morality, however, requires an intensity bordering on hysteria. Mary Eberstadt has recently updated some of Bloom's themes by arguing that the collective shriek of identity politics draws much of its energy from the collapse of the family, for which it

---

320  Stanley Kurtz, "Culture and Values in the 1960s," in Peter Berkowitz ed., *Never a Matter of Indifference: Sustaining Virtue in a Free Republic*, (Stanford: Stanford University Press, 2003), pp. 29-55.
321  Peter Wood, Michael Toscano, *What Does Bowdoin Teach? How a Contemporary Liberal Arts College Shapes Students*, (New York: National Association of Scholars, April 3, 2013), https://www.nas.org/blogs/dicta/what_does_bowdoin_teach_how_a_contemporary_liberal_arts_college_shapes_stud

imperfectly substitutes. We can now add that the moral minimalism of identity politics requires constant outrage as well because the game only works when ultimate offenses like racism and genocide are at stake.

Students for Environmental and Racial Justice (SERJ), a new intersectional group formed at Stanford in 2019, covers both bases. Tucked away on Stanford's bucolic campus, SERJ's leaders speak as if from the bowels of the death star. They blame Leland Stanford for stealing the school's land from the Indians; perpetuating an Indian genocide as California's governor; and decimating the buffalo as president of the Central Pacific Railroad.[322] SERJ seeks to disabuse students of the belief that their university benefits society at large. Stanford, to them, is a cog in the "global power machine," training the ruling class to profit from the "social and material death of poor people." Life on earth, according to SERJ, is in the midst of a "major extinction" the effects of which are already being felt by indigenous, colonized, and oppressed peoples. This extinction is the supposed aim of what SERJ views as the ultimate enemy: "Christological Racial Capitalism." With Earth on the verge of ecological collapse, SERJ's solution is inversion of the world order. Colonizing nations must atone for their social, cultural, and environmental crimes by embracing "reparations frameworks" and shifting sovereignty and power back to global indigenous peoples.

Stanford, according to SERJ, lacks even the language that would allow it to grasp these truths. And so it must pay reparations and place the school's newly initiated long-range planning process in the hands of students who are black, indigenous, and of color. SERJ mocks Stanford's current leadership, as well as its pretentions to institutional continuity:

> Many elite higher education institutions are kept afloat by large teams of venture capitalists, working to ensure institutional existence into perpetuity…This is an actual goal of the board of trustees: that Stanford exists into perpetuity…as if anything can exist into perpetuity…[323]

---

322 Maya Burke, Gabriel Saiz, Nathaniel Ramos, Nancy Chang, Ayoade Balogun, Whitney Francis, Anna Greene, "The Time to Act was Yesterday: Private Institutions & Environmental Justice," *The Stanford Daily*, April 12, 2019, https://www.stanforddaily.com/2019/04/12/the-time-to-act-was-yesterday-private-institutions-environmental-justice/

323 Ibid.

Anything but colonial guilt, that is. Institutions are fragile and illusory social constructions; the Western Civ teaching tradition is a lie; but the guilt of ancient oppressors apparently lives on forever.

SERJ apportions guilt by skin-color, too, whether the immigrant ancestors of white Stanford students lived in America during the Gold Rush or not. Innocence is skin deep as well. South Asian students are eligible to be on the committees that ought to be guiding Stanford's future, whether Leland Stanford stole South Asian land or not. It's enough that the British East India Company might have done so in the eighteenth century.

The bugaboo of today's academy is "essentialism," the sin of overgeneralizing, in which a common characteristic is attributed to some class of people (men, women, heterosexuals, homosexuals, or a racial or ethnic group), or continuity is claimed for some institution (any given nation or civilization). Overgeneralization is surely a problem, yet everyone "essentializes" because language and thought are impossible without generalization of some kind. That is why, in a fleeting moment of honesty, postmodernists came up with the idea of "strategic essentialism," by which favored political groups give themselves permission to generalize—and overgeneralize—for approved political purposes.

SERJ is teaching a veritable master-class in strategic essentialism, mocking Stanford's very real and impressive institutional continuity while magically essentializing a simplistic version of history across barriers of time, race, and culture.

The overheated tone—the visions of racism, genocide, and planetary extinction in the midst of Stanford's seemingly beneficent scientific, medical, and technical prowess—is no less than what is required if moral minimalism is going to satisfy its disciples. Literally saving the world can substitute for the old civilizational, religious, national, communal, and familial norms of sacrifice only as long as the apocalypse remains plausible. Even global salvation won't fill the gap, however, once these young activists form families, and children raise the stakes. Then again, families aren't being formed as quickly or as often anymore. Nowadays, climate activists even pledge to forego children.

When SERJ formed in April of 2019, it sponsored a student walkout. Protestors demanding a joining of environmental and racial justice marched across Stanford's campus shouting: "Whose land is this? Ohlone land...Black, Indigenous, POC hands, all over Stanford's long-range plans."[324] So 1987's chants of "Hey hey, ho ho, Western Culture's got to go," have been replaced thirty-two years later by demands for race-based control of the school. In the absence of a cultural commonality capable of inspiring mutual obligation and sacrifice, racial alliances and animosities are all that remain to lend collective purpose. (For more on the quasi-religious valence of campus environmentalism, see Rachelle Peterson and Peter Wood's NAS report, *Sustainability: Higher Education's New Fundamentalism*.)[325]

## Grave-Digging

It is possible now to understand how the fashionable deconstructionism launched by scholars like Gilbert Allardyce helped give rise to overwrought and continually expanding charges of racism, and why such charges have moved to the nation's center stage. Allardyce was a creature of the sixties, with its newly radicalized individualism. As a junior scholar, he helped bring down Stanford's original Western Civ requirement by rebelliously teaching his section of the course along the lines of his individual interests. He thought he was deepening the course when instead, to use his own words, he was "digging its grave." Allardyce no more sacrificed his individual interests to a common civilizational or national project than his generational colleagues would fight a war they didn't believe in. As their writings make clear, it wasn't just the Vietnam War that baby boomer radicals rejected, but the very reality of civilizations, cultures, and national traditions.

Uprooted from family and community after high school, the baby boomers attended college in unprecedented numbers. Even their upbringing in suburbs and increasingly anonymous cities represented a break from the small towns and tightly-knit ethnic urban neighborhoods of the previous generation.[326] Living a more individualist life than

---

324 Elise Miller, "Environmental justice rally demands faculty, reparations, agency," *The Stanford Daily*, April 16, 2019, https://www.stanforddaily.com/2019/04/16/environmental-justice-rally-demands-faculty-reparations-agency/
325 Rachelle Peterson, Peter Wood, *Sustainability: Higher Education's New Fundamentalism*, (New York: National Association of Scholars, 2015), https://www.nas.org/blogs/dicta/sustainability_higher_educations_new_fundamentalism1
326 Alan Ehrenhalt, *The Lost City: The Forgotten Virtues Of Community in America*, (New York: Basic Books, 1995); Christopher Lasch, *The True and Only Heaven: Progress and Its Critics*, (New York: W. W. Norton & Co., 1991).

any previous cohort of Americans, the baby boomers saw through some of the naïveté and illusions of the old civilizational and national traditions, and of some of the scholarship that celebrated these as well.

Yet Allardyce and his generational colleagues had their own characteristic blind spots. As community and family declined, cultural continuity came to be denied and debunked every bit as uncritically as it had been affirmed in an earlier age. For increasing numbers of boomers, social institutions as sustaining traditions that amount to more than the sum of their parts had become unbelievable. Yet this suspicion was, in great part, an artifact of the post-World War II era.

In the new intellectual dispensation, traditions were simultaneously deconstructed and excoriated. Civilizations, religions, nations, and families became oppressors and illusions all at once. Globalization was waved like a wand at hated or embarrassing traditions to make them disappear. Yet the idea of globalization makes no sense, and can neither be traced nor measured, without assessing its progress against the very traditions it has been used to deconstruct. The theory does not cohere, except perhaps as the rage, incomprehension, and yearning of generations for whom families and communities have disintegrated. Allardyce's debunking of the Western Civ teaching tradition has the additional defect of being just plain wrong. How many other deconstructive conceits are similarly mistaken? We won't know until the disciplines confront the new deconstructionist orthodoxy with the skepticism now reserved for the (no longer) "dominant narrative."

Bloom knew all about scholarly debunking of the American founding on historicist, pragmatist, and Marxist premises.[327] This is what convinced him that the intellectual underpinnings of the American experiment had already been hollowed out in the eyes of the country's elite. Yet Allardyce's subversion of the very idea of continuous tradition was an advance over old-style debunking, and particularly-suited to a hyper-individualist age. The Allardyce thesis was a new instantiation of Tocqueville's atomized individual randomly caroming through time. Allardyce's skepticism about the very existence of tradition was an early instance of what would eventually mount into an avalanche of historical deconstructionism. Yet with continuous traditions of all sorts now in doubt, expanded accusations of racism rather than nihilist paralysis became the order of the day.

---

327 Bloom, *Closing*, p. 56.

# Stripped of Their Cultures

Stanford's Western Culture controversy is famous for having introduced "multiculturalism" to America. Use of the word took off a few years after the battle, but the great Stanford curriculum clash injected the substance of what would come to be called multiculturalism into public debate in 1988. No-one could define multiculturalism straightforwardly. We've seen that what multiculturalism meant changed with the ever-shifting interests of its advocates. Should members of non-Western cultures be treated equally, or permitted to disregard and even challenge American norms? It depends on its advocates' interests of the moment—and woe to those who guess wrong.

For all this confusion, it seemed clear at least that "culture" was the heart of the matter. And indeed, classic cultural relativism was often invoked in defense of "multiculturalism." Yet "culture" was never much more than the appealing but superficial surface of this movement. It would have been more accurate to call the phenomenon "anti-culturalism." That's because so-called multiculturalism was always a way of building a coalition under a rubric of "oppression." And oppression as a common denominator serves only to diminish the rich and varied social forms traditionally designated by the word "culture." The gradual shift away from "multiculturalism" to the term "intersectionality"—meaning intersecting forms of oppression—implicitly acknowledges the misdirection of the original name. By reducing cultural difference to a quantum of oppression to be ranked and calculated for any given individual or group, intersectionality actually strips cultures of their divergent content and converts their erstwhile participants into individuals bereft of meaning or direction outside the league of the oppressed.

Members of the multicultural, or now, intersectional coalition may be slowly stripped of their cultures. Yet they do have a place in history, or rather, a new history is constructed in place of the old—a history of oppression in which culture plays but a minor role, if any. If postmodern historical skepticism makes sense anywhere, it is here. The historical essentialisms imaginatively constructed by the putatively oppressed of our day are nothing if not ripe for deconstruction. Back when Western civilization still seemed worth taking credit for, minorities drew on questionable Afrocentrist scholarship to claim that Plato and Aristotle had stolen their ideas from dark-skinned ancient Egyptians. Allardyce and scholars of his generation constructed an imaginative history in which warmongering leaders had hoodwinked college students during World War I with the same lie about Western civilization they deployed to justify Vietnam. Today's Latinx students erase hundreds of years of Latin American culture—their own heritage—by reimagining themselves as indigenous pre-Columbians rejecting oppressive European norms.

This is collective denial. And what is being denied is the influence of Western individualism on the core convictions of American minorities and radical professors alike. Invented historical essentialisms notwithstanding, campus radicals can still find the sources of their aspirations and dilemmas in the Western classics. They are descendants of Western civilization, whether they believe it or not. Not "white glorification" but self-knowledge flows from the Western classics, skin color notwithstanding. Since the days of Robertson and Guizot, the story of the West has been a tale of advancing individualism, and for good or ill, today's left is writing the latest chapter. Imagined communities have their effects, but Western civilization lives on in the souls of Americans, whether we acknowledge it or not.

Yet the very real and continuing influence of Western and American culture on students-in-denial cannot, by itself, forestall the next phase. The rejection of the Western tradition on grounds of skin color means that many Westerners now define themselves first and foremost by race. That view is already taking its toll. Race is the new culture—thin, problematic, and unsatisfactory as a replacement for our richer collective traditions. Racial conflict driven by forces little understood increasingly seems to be our national fate. The mutual incomprehension and dearth of common symbols foreseen and welcomed by Mary Louise Pratt in the aftermath of Stanford's Western culture controversy is emerging. This is not primarily a function of failed assimilation (although assimilation continues as an important issue and a challenge). The deeper problem is that ever-more Americans are assimilating to a common conviction that racism is the crucial controlling reality of America's past and present.

The dominant force within Stanford's intersectional alliance is the Students of Color Coalition. Stanford's "Who's Teaching Us?" alliance wants to replace courses about culture with classes centered on anti-oppression scholarship and "people of color frameworks." In cultural terms, there is no basis for a "people of color framework." On the contrary, the varied cultures at play in a typical intersectional coalition are profoundly different, even clashing. The prime thing bringing these cultures together is skin color and, it is posited, a common history of oppression at the hands of Western whites. Turning "people of color" into the controlling framework of history and contemporary society alike is both intellectually superficial and a recipe for irreconcilable national division, and worse.

Bloom's ungrounded students lacked any shared or solid basis for choosing how to live. Race is the opposite of that. Race is (or at least superficially appears to be) written into the structure of life, an ineradicable choice made for us by fate. Under the guise of fighting racism, race has seduced its acolytes into turning "color" into a life-plan and a reason for being, filling the existential gap.

## Admit It or Not

Thirty-some years ago, Stanford launched a two-pronged attack on Western Culture. The Allardyce thesis was invoked to debunk the idea that teaching Western Civ and its founding texts was a revered and longstanding tradition. Instruction in Western history was supposedly little more than a bogus propaganda device, a twentieth century invention designed to hoodwink naïve young Americans into putting their lives on the line in Europe. Simultaneously, Stanford's Rainbow Alliance, led by the Black Students Union, charged that requiring students to read the Western great books was racist, and so was any student who advocated or even studied a great books curriculum. The Western Culture requirement was decried as "not just racist education but the education of racists." From the start, then, deconstructionist historical skepticism and expansive accusations of racism operated in tandem. The Stanford Western Culture controversy was arguably the first time that either academic deconstructionism or sweeping accusations of racism detached from conscious intention had broken into public debate.

The arms of this pincer attack were strategically coordinated and compatible. The message of the Allardyce thesis was that Western Civ was a late arrival whose sell-by date had just passed. Western Civ may have made some modest sense in an era when European immigrants needed assimilating, but that era was supposedly over. The Afrocentric revival and growing immigration from outside the West meant that requiring Western Civ of all Stanford students was impermissibly ethnocentric (and to all intents and purposes "racist"). Ultimately, then, the Allardyce thesis as deployed by Stanford's radical scholars and the racism accusations hurled by the Rainbow Alliance were one and the same.

Skeptical deconstructive history and the moral certainties of the new racial politics have been working in tandem ever since, in more ways than one. By keeping students of non-Western descent (do American blacks even fit this category?) out of Western Civ, multiculturalists make it nearly impossible to achieve a common American culture. That, of course, is the goal. Yet the irony is that campus multiculturalists are Western individualists whether they admit it or not.

And now the alliance of skeptical deconstructionism and student intersectionality has deprived even non-minority students of access to a common Western tradition. For starters, Western Civ requirements are dead. The one-time flood is down to a trickle. More deeply, a multicultural reading of the Western tradition now dominates the academy. When Pratt dismissed America's constitutional liberties as a ruse of America's powerful white European elite, she was an outlier. Her view is entirely familiar today. Americans, as a result, are either discouraged from studying their own tradition or tempted to misread it through the lens of white identity politics. In the eyes of some, white identity politics is everywhere already. For others, we're nowhere near that point and it's the false accusations that are tearing us apart instead.

## A New American Culture

These dynamics have spilled out of the academy and into the center of our culture. When President Trump defends Western Civilization or speaks of American greatness, he's attacked by a now predominant multiculturalist left for speaking in racist code.[328] Many candidates for the 2020 Democratic presidential nomination condemn America's "systemic racism," and the *New York Times* has even launched a project to make that case.[329] Conservatives, of course, demur. It's as

---

328  Cody Derespina, "Trump defends Western Civilization—and media call it racist," Fox News, July 7, 2017, https://www.foxnews.com/politics/trump-defends-western-civilization-and-media-call-it-racist; Issac Bailey, "Why Trump's MAGA hats have become a potent symbol of racism," CNN, March 12, 2019, https://www.cnn.com/2019/01/21/opinions/maga-hat-has-become-a-potent-racist-symbol-bailey/index.html
329  Natalie Allison, "'This country was founded on white supremacy': Beto O'Rourke speaks with Tennessee immigrants," Nashville Tennesseean, July 8, 2019, https://www.tennessean.com/story/news/politics/2019/07/08/beto-orourke-nashville-tennessee-visit-gathers-immigrants-white-supremacy-raids-deten-

though the Stanford campus culture wars of 1988 have gone national. Jesse Jackson's gentle image of the many-colored quilt, offered when multiculturalism was still confined to the political sidelines, seems very far away.

At the cutting edge of campus intersectionality's extra-academic advance we find "The Squad," the alliance of four left-leaning congresswomen of color—Alexandria Ocasio-Cortez, Ilhan Omar, Rashida Tlaib, and Ayanna Pressley. The Squad serves as a lightning rod for the clash between multiculturalism and a more traditional conception of America. It isn't necessary to pick through their politics to recognize that the Squad hews to the main lines of campus intersectionality.

Pressley is known for saying, "We don't need any more brown faces that don't want to be a brown voice. We don't need black faces that don't want to be a black voice. We don't need Muslims that don't want to be a Muslim voice. We don't need queers that don't want to be a queer voice."[330] Beyond being an ultimate exercise in "intragroup marginalization," Pressley, a black woman, is here demanding group solidarity not only from blacks but from "browns" (Latinxs?), Muslims, and "queers." The implication is that all of these seemingly varied cultural voices sing from the same oppression-themed hymnal. And although the racial element in Pressley's remarks is tempered by the addition of "queers," the overall thrust of her exhortation is to oppose "people of color" to whites.

When Rashida Tlaib and Ilhan Omar were challenged by American conservatives to condemn a Palestinian Authority ban on LGBTQ activities within the West Bank, they responded by criticizing the ban, but also by arguing that the issue shouldn't distract from the larger evil of Israel's occupation. The congresswomen quoted statements by the Palestinian LGBTQ group Al-Qaws to the effect that Israel's occupation actually contributes to the suppression of Palestinian LGBTQs. They also echoed Al-Qaws's claim that "colonialism, patriarchy, and homophobia are all connected forms of oppression."[331] Without wading

---

tion-centers/1675044001/; Karma Allen, "Democrats tackle racism, mass incarceration on debate stage," ABC News, September 12, 2019, https://abcnews.go.com/Politics/democrats-tackle-racism-mass-incarceration-debate-stage/story?id=65583080; Matthew Desmond, "The 1619 Project," *The New York Times*, August 14, 2019, https://www.nytimes.com/interactive/2019/08/14/magazine/1619-america-slavery.html

330  Rebecca Klar, "Pressley: Democrats don't need 'any more black faces that don't want to be a black voice,'" *The Hill*, July 14, 2019, https://thehill.com/homenews/house/453007-pressley-democrats-need-any-more-black-voices-that-dont-want-to-be-a-black

331  Menachem Shlomo, "Ilhan Omar, Rashida Tlaib Respond to Palestinian Authority's LGBTQ Ban," *The Jerusalem Post*, August 20, 2019, https://www.jpost.com/Israel-News/Ilhan-Omar-Rashida-Tlaib-respond-to-Palestinian-LGBTQ-ban-on-Twitter-599139

into the substance of this controversy, it's evident that Omar and Tlaib share the intersectional ideology and line up with LGBTQs rather than traditional Muslim culture on issues of sexuality, when push comes to shove.

Alexandria Ocasio-Cortez is known for preferring Latinx to Latino and very much thinks in terms of "people of color." Perhaps her most controversial move to date was to suggest that House Speaker Nancy Pelosi had been "outright disrespectful" for explicitly singling out "newly elected women of color" (i.e. The Squad) for criticism.[332] For many, the implication of Ocasio-Cortez's remarks was that Speaker Pelosi is a racist. Was Pelosi singling out the Squad for criticism on racial grounds, or was the Squad unfairly construing the ordinary give-and-take of politics as racism? As campus intersectionality seeps further into the culture, we will likely be revisiting this debate again and again. On campus, and now in the halls of Congress, culture in the traditional sense has given way to endless disputes over race. Accusations of racism are becoming the new American culture.

Radical, post-sixties individualism dissolves traditional communities, nowadays including even the community built around our core civilizational ideals and shared constitutional principles. Skeptical postmodern academic thinking is the intellectual branch of this project of cultural deconstruction. Oddly, however, quasi-nihilistic academic skepticism works in tandem with the moral certainties of intersectional politics. As faith in shared national and civilizational ideals goes by the boards, opposition to racism, bigotry, and genocide are all we've got left. That works, until crusades around these issues are artificially ginned up to fill the hollow space where traditional religion, nation, community, morality, and family used to be. Intersectional crusades around our moral bottom lines tend to strip the last remaining elements of traditional cultures and communities away, leaving us with competing alliances based on skin color, overwrought tales of oppression, and little else.

Stanford's administration denied that anything much was at stake in the 1988 controversy over its Western Culture requirement. Critics and defenders of the course knew better. Can there be a transnational national culture and can it be good? What happens to our constitutional

---

332 Justin Wise, "Ocasio-Cortez accuses Pelosi of 'persistent singling out' of women of color: It's 'outright disrespectful,'" *The Hill*, July 10, 2019, https://thehill.com/homenews/house/452546-ocasio-cortez-accuses-pelosi-of-persistent-singling-out-women-of-color-its

fabric when John Locke is replaced by Franz Fanon? These were the questions of three decades past, and the answers are increasingly clear. A transnational national culture means the end of nation and culture as we know them and the start of a clash based on race instead. Fanon was a theorist of violent racial conflict. Swapping Locke for Fanon leaves race as the preferred framework for social connection—and for group skirmishing as well. "Imagine there's no countries, etc.," turns out to be a formula for anomie and racial antagonism. The American idea offers a way out of the race trap for those willing to take it. In its absence, unfortunately, there emerges no "brotherhood of man." Without a common civilizational and national culture, the way is open to racial finger-pointing instead. A Lennonist universal society, even if it could be achieved, would likely be as culturally flat, ideologically uniform, and aggressively thought-policed as Stanford's intersectional coalition.

Unlikely as it seems, it's still not too late to return to Western civilization and the common national culture that a common heritage informs. We can return to the West because we've never really left it. Our strengths and our weaknesses are Western, because Western is what Americans are—"people of color" included. Step one is to restore and recover the history we've abandoned under an avalanche of deconstructive skepticism. Foolishly, we've accepted that skepticism on faith. The evidence now suggests this faith was misplaced.

# Index

# Index

Adams, Herbert Baxter 32, 34, 41, 43, 45
Adams, John 20, 33, 64
Adams, John Quincy 33, 35
Africa 18, 22, 32, 91
African 67, 96, 104, 106, 110
Afrocentric 140
Afrocentrist 138
Allardyce
   Allardyce, Gilbert 10, 11, 19-21, 25, 29, 35, 41, 42, 45-53, 55-62, 64, 70, 73-79, 82, 83, 85, 87, 88-90, 92, 93, 95, 103, 106, 109, 111, 128, 136-138, 140
   Allardyce thesis 10, 19, 20, 21, 25, 47, 48, 51, 53, 58, 59, 61, 64, 73, 76, 82, 85, 88, 89, 90, 92, 93, 106, 128, 137, 140
American exceptionalism. See Exceptionalism: American Exceptionalism
AP European History 73, 88-90
   APEH 89, 90
AP U.S. History 88, 89
   APUSH 89
Aristotle 100, 133, 138
Assimilation 38, 68, 75, 95, 120, 139
   assimilated 108, 123
   assimilationist 76, 79
Atlantic World 18


Beauvoir, Simone de 116
Bennett, William 102
Bernard, J. S. 39, 45, 50
Bernard, L. L. 39, 45, 50
Bible 47, 81, 100
   Biblical 115
Black Student Union (Stanford) 101
Bloom, Allen 11, 20, 35, 66, 84, 85, 124-133, 137, 140
Brexit 92
Bush, George W. 25
Byrnes, Robert 56, 58, 60


Capitalism 18, 61, 89, 109
Catholic 38, 69, 115, 116, 119
Channing, Edward 60
Charles V 27-30, 32, 34
China 22, 24, 106
Christendom 21-23, 36, 63
Christianity 22, 24, 29, 38, 69, 89
   Christian 19, 21-23, 38, 45, 63, 69, 104, 116, 123
Cicero 64, 65, 66

cisgender 110, 114-116
College Board 18, 73, 88-90
colonialism 53, 80, 103, 109, 131, 142
    colonial 10, 18, 24, 70, 89, 104, 106, 111, 113, 114, 123, 125, 134
    colonizing 134
Columbia 46, 56, 58, 59, 60, 61, 81, 112
constructivist 70, 78, 80, 81, 83
continuity 23, 29, 46, 50-52, 55, 63, 64, 66-68, 79, 82, 95, 111, 123, 128, 134-136
    continuous 52, 55, 66, 78, 79, 137
Coolidge, Archibald Cary 55-60, 62
Cornell University 45, 126, 130
Crusades 29
Culture, Ideas, and Values (course) 77, 83, 84, 89, 107, 111


Darwin, Charles 46, 100
deconstructionism 10, 67, 82, 136, 137, 140
    deconstruction 18, 64, 82, 86, 88, 92, 138, 143
    deconstructionist 9, 11, 17, 18, 52, 67, 88, 92, 112, 123, 137, 140
    deconstructionist history 17, 123
    deconstructive 18, 19, 20, 95, 137, 140, 144
Diamond, Larry 118
diffusionism 92
    diffusionist 92
divorce 128


Eberstadt, Mary 133
Edwards, Jonathan 21, 22, 26, 63
Egypt 106, 107
eighties 77, 125-128, 130
    1980s 65, 66, 76-79, 96, 100, 125-128
elective system 48-51, 60
    elective 48-52, 60
Eliot, Charles William 43, 49, 51-53, 65, 66, 69
Elliott, Harry 107, 108, 110, 111, 117, 123
England 18, 22, 24, 31, 39, 40, 69
English exceptionalist 40
Enlightenment 19, 21, 23, 26-28, 30, 31, 33, 34, 54, 64-66
essentialism 82, 86, 95, 111, 114, 135
European civilization 22, 23, 28, 29, 33, 36-40, 43, 46-48, 54, 55, 62, 63, 65
Exceptionalism 20, 22, 29, 36, 40, 44, 46-48, 68-70
    American exceptionalism 20, 22, 29, 40, 44, 46-48, 68-70
    exceptional 24, 44, 69, 130
    exceptionalist 22, 36, 40, 44, 46-48, 68
expanded charge of racism 99
    expanded racism charge 102

family 18, 38, 99, 115-117, 119, 126-128, 133, 136, 143
Fanon, Frantz 84, 85, 143, 144
Felton, Cornelius Conway 36, 42, 54, 55, 65
Ferguson, Adam 26, 27, 31, 32, 33, 42, 47, 53, 54, 63, 65
Foucault, Michel 78-80, 86, 91, 95, 103, 111, 131, 132
   Foucauldian 103, 111, 131, 132
France 30, 36-41, 54, 69, 79
free speech 110


Gay 127
general education 49, 62, 74, 76, 79, 88
genocide 11, 133-135, 143
George III 30, 53
globalization 17, 67, 76, 83, 84, 86, 91, 92, 107, 137
   global 11, 12, 18, 22, 76, 88, 91, 92, 109, 117, 134, 135
   globalist 11, 18-20, 67, 73, 90, 91, 95
   globalized 10, 67, 89, 90
   globalizing 15, 16, 17, 61, 67, 76, 79, 84
Goethe 65
Great Books 26, 51, 52, 64, 65, 80, 83
   great works 15, 75, 79, 81
Greek Revolution 35
groundlessness 127, 128, 133
Groundlessness
   groundless 133
Guizot, Francois 10, 36-50, 54, 55, 60, 62, 63, 65-69, 75, 139


Hartman, Andrew 59, 62
Harvard 31-33, 36, 42-45, 48-52, 54-58, 60, 64, 66, 96, 97
Herodotus 23, 42, 65, 106
Hispanic 76, 112, 114, 120
Homer 26, 51, 64, 65
humanities 10-12, 42, 43, 46, 59, 74, 76, 77, 79, 81, 83, 107, 119, 120, 124
Hume, David 28, 68


identity politics 10, 91, 98, 113, 122, 133, 141
"Imagine" by John Lennon 15, 17, 25, 144
immigration 38, 76, 79, 83, 84, 87, 88, 117, 130, 140
   immigrants 20, 68, 70, 75, 76, 104, 123, 140, 141
imperialism 101, 104, 113, 115, 124, 125
   imperialist 53, 95, 100, 103, 104, 112
individualist 110, 115, 116, 124, 125, 136, 137
   individualist 110, 115, 116, 124, 125, 136, 137
informal curriculum 31, 32
intersectionality 11, 87, 113, 116, 117, 120, 123, 138, 141-143

intersectional 117-119, 123, 125, 130, 131, 134, 138, 139, 142-144
intragroup marginalization 121-123, 129, 142
invent 46, 79
Israel 19, 117-119, 142


Jackson, Jesse 96-98, 105, 142
Jefferson, Thomas 20, 34, 44, 64, 66
Johnson, Lyndon 99
Junkerman, Charles 84


Kaufman, Elliot 110, 111, 117, 118, 123, 130
Kemp, Amanda 101, 102, 108
Kennedy, John F. 74
knowledge 26, 28, 31, 57, 78, 79, 92, 95, 104, 111, 132, 139
Kreeger, Joanna 109


Latina 115, 116, 118, 119
Latin America 87, 113, 115
Latin American 113, 115, 116, 138
Latino 112-114, 116, 119-123, 143
Latinx 112-116, 119, 123, 125, 138, 143
Lennon, John (Lennonism, Lennonist) 15, 17, 92
Levine, Lawrence 20, 26, 31-35, 41, 42, 44-50, 58-60, 68, 88, 90
LGBTQ+ 112, 127, 142
liberalism 110, 116, 124, 131, 132
Lindenberger, Herbert 81-83, 86, 88, 96
Locke, John 65, 84, 85, 116, 143, 144
Lopez, J. Derek 120-123, 130
Lougee, Carolyn 74-77, 79, 81, 83, 89, 90
Louis XIV 30
Lynn, Erika 109


Madison, James 26, 33, 34, 65
marginal 78, 117
  marginalization 119, 121-123, 129, 142
  marginalized 111, 117, 118
Marxism 91, 129
  Marxist 40, 88, 89, 111, 137
Marx, Karl 37, 41, 46, 65, 79, 81, 100, 116
McGuffey, William 46, 47, 49
memorization 20, 26, 32, 35, 36, 42, 57, 64
Merkel, Angela 16
millennial(s) 127
Mill, John Stuart 37, 40, 43, 65

mismatch 121-123, 129
Missouri, University of 46, 113
Monroe, James 35
Montesquieu 23-26, 31-34, 40, 42, 63, 66, 69
Moral Majority 126, 127
Moral Minimalism 131
Morgan, Lewis Henry 46, 47, 69
Moynihan, Daniel Patrick 99, 100-103
multicultural 9, 67, 76, 86, 95, 98, 108, 111, 116, 118, 124, 138
Muslim 39, 106, 119, 123, 130, 142


New York Times 15, 76, 88, 101, 102, 141
non-binary 112, 114
Norton, Charles Eliot 43, 51-55, 60, 62, 65, 66, 69, 91, 136


Obama, Barack 98, 99
Ocasio-Cortez, Alexandria 142, 143
Omar, Ilhan 142
oppression 97, 104, 105, 106, 109-111, 116, 117, 119, 120, 123, 125, 126, 138, 139, 142, 143
  oppressed 95, 105, 118, 119, 134, 138
Orientalism, by Edward Said 103, 104, 111


people of color 119, 120, 125, 139, 142-144
  PoC 120
Persephone, Abigail 109
philhellenes 66
  philhellenic 65
Plato 65, 81, 100, 133, 138
political correctness 73, 86, 99
postcolonial 82, 103, 111
postmodern 12, 54, 73, 84, 96, 103, 114, 138, 143
power 22, 25, 27, 29, 30, 31, 34, 39, 40, 41, 48, 53, 62, 70, 78, 92, 95, 98, 103, 104, 105, 110-112, 117-120, 123, 131, 132, 134
Pratt, Mary Louise 64, 83-88, 90, 91, 96, 139, 141
Pressley, Ayanna 142
Princeton 21, 22, 26, 32, 34, 35, 51, 54, 58, 64, 66
Protestant 21
Providence 28, 30, 63
Pufendorf, Samuel von 22


racism 9, 11, 80, 84, 95, 97, 99, 101-108, 119-123, 126, 130-133, 135-137, 139-141, 143
  racist 95, 100-103, 105, 106, 108, 121, 122, 131, 140, 141, 143

rainbow agenda 97
Rainbow Alliance 103, 106, 117, 130, 140
Rainbow Coalition 96-98, 102
regime of truth 78-80, 95
　Also see Foucault, Michel
relativism 37, 38, 82, 86, 110, 112, 115, 123-125, 129, 130, 131, 133, 138
　relativist 9, 25, 38, 61, 82, 95, 110, 124, 131
rising American electorate 98
Roberts, Jon H. 51
Robertson, William 10, 27, 28
Robinson, James Harvey 59, 60-62
Roosevelt, Franklin D. 57


sacrality 81
Sacrality
　sacred 81, 100
　sanctity 83
Said, Edward 103, 104, 111, 123
Scotland 27, 31
　Scottish 26, 27, 30, 34, 54
　Scotts 34
Segal, Daniel 58, 60-62, 74, 90
Sepsey, Loralee 107-109
SERJ. See Students for Environmental and Racial Justice
Shakespeare, William 26, 51, 65
Sheehan, Colleen 33, 34
Siedentop, Larry 37-40
Siegel, Thomas J. 31-33
sixties 98, 104, 126, 128, 131, 132, 136, 143
Sixties
　1960s 61, 73, 74, 79, 96, 126, 133
Smith, Bonnie 90
SOCC. See Students of Color Coalition
Spanish 21, 22, 53, 83, 86, 113, 114
Sparks, Jared 42-45, 49, 54, 66
Spivak, Gayatri Chakravorty 82, 86
Squad, The 142, 143
Staloff, Darren 33
Stanford, Leland 134, 135
Stanford Review (magazine) 107-111, 116-119
Stanford University 9, 15, 25, 73, 102, 133
Stearns, Peter 89, 90
strategic essentialism 82, 86, 111, 114, 135
Students for Environmental and Racial Justice 134
Students of Color Coalition 117, 119, 139
third gender 114
Third World 83, 84, 88, 125
Thucydides 42, 65

Tlaib, Rashida 142
Tocqueville, Alexis de 37, 40, 41, 43, 44, 67, 69, 116, 128, 137
Torrey, Henry W. 49, 60
Trump, Donald 15, 92, 141
Turner, James 43, 51-55


Varouxakis, Georgios 40
Vietnam 19, 128, 136, 138
Voltaire 28-30, 34, 81, 100


Wall Street Journal 84, 85, 106, 124, 127
War 9, 10, 19, 22, 23, 27, 30, 34-36, 44, 45, 47-53, 56, 58-62, 67, 68, 70, 73, 75, 76, 79, 88, 118, 136, 137, 138
War Issues (course) 19, 56, 61
White, Andrew Dickson 44, 46, 50
white identity politics 10, 141
white supremacy 86, 109, 132, 141
Who's Teaching Us (organzation) 110, 111, 120, 125, 139
Winterer, Caroline 21, 34-36, 49, 50, 65
Winthrop, John 22
Witherspoon, John 26, 27, 32, 34, 35
World War I 10, 19, 34-36, 44, 47, 48, 50- 52, 56, 58-62, 67, 68, 73, 76, 88, 138
  First World War 10, 23, 53, 55, 56, 58, 60, 61, 70, 75, 79
  Great War 49, 60
WTU. See Who's Teaching Us (organzation)


Yale University 21, 46, 113, 129